WHAT OTHERS ARE SAYING ABOUT *EXCUSE ME, YOUR SOUL MATE IS WAITING*

Excuse Me, Your Soul Mate Is Waiting is an excellent addition to the field of relationships. In this exceptional and fun read, Marla combines the metaphysical teachings of using the Law of Attraction with her years of expertise in the matchmaking field to help you navigate through the dating world and find the love of your life. Enjoy this book . . . and let it help you find your own soul mate!

—John Gray, PhD, author of *Men Are from Mars, Women Are from Venus* and *The Mars & Venus Diet & Exercise Solution*

In *Excuse Me, Your Soul Mate Is Waiting*, Marla has put together a truly unique and important book on the best possible way to find the love of your life. It's exciting to find that we possess the power within ourselves to draw in that special someone, and this book will empower you to take control of your destiny. Marla combines her expertise as a matchmaker and her knowledge of metaphysics in a unique magical combination, along with humor to guide you on the path to your soul mate. After reading this book, you will know that you have the power to use the Law of Attraction to get into the right relationship and not wait around for fate or luck to bring you the love of your life.

—Ellen Fein and Sherrie Schneider, co-authors of *The Rule*

D0200103

The combination of Marla's message that you have the power to use the Law of Attraction to find your soul mate and her practical advice to keep him once he's here is a refreshing twist in a relationship book.

—Nina Siemaszko, actress, *The West Wing*

With wit and wisdom, *Excuse Me, Your Soul Mate Is Waiting* gives you just the right tools to attract the perfect partner into your life in a fun and effortless way. Follow the steps in this book, and you will be buzzing away with such great energy that even if your soul mate hasn't arrived yet, you will become a highly attractive person and be having the time of your life!

—Dr. Lisa Love, author of *Beyond the Secret: Spiritual Power and the Law of Attraction*

This book beautifully combines looking for love with the Law of Attraction, and how it can lead you to the love of your life. Marla's book will help you identify the qualities you want in your soul mate and how to attract this person to you. It is a must-read for anyone looking to find his or her soul mate.

—Helen Gray, life coach

This is a delightful book! Informative, insightful, wise, entertaining, and a lot of fun.

—Doug Fieger, lead singer of *The Knack*

Excuse Me, Your Soul Mate Is Waiting

Marla Martenson

HAMPTON ROADS
PUBLISHING COMPANY, INC.

Cover design by Bookwrights Design

Hampton Roads Publishing Company, Inc.
1125 Stoney Ridge Road
Charlottesville, VA 22902

434-296-2772
fax: 434-296-5096
e-mail: hrpc@hrpub.com
www.hrpub.com

If you are unable to order this book from your local
bookseller, you may order directly from the publisher.
Call 1-800-766-8009, toll-free.

Library of Congress Cataloging-in-Publication Data
Martenson, Marla.
Excuse me, your soul mate is waiting / Marla Martenson.
    p. cm.
Summary: "A professional matchmaker teaches people how to
find their soul
mates using the Law of Attraction"--Provided by publisher.
  ISBN-13: 978-1-57174-560-6 (5.5 x 8.5 tp : alk. paper)
  1. Mate selection. 2. Soul mates. 3. Dating (Social customs) I.
Title.
  HQ801.M373 2008
  646.7'7--dc22
                            2007039782

ISBN 978-1-57174-560-6

10 9 8 7 6 5 4 3 2 1

Printed on acid-free paper in the United States
Note: The names and background information of all people in this
book have been changed to sufficiently protect their identities.

This book is dedicated with deepest love and affection to my husband, Adolfo Bringas. His support, creative inspiration, and patience have supported me to achieve my new endeavors. And this book is also dedicated to all the singles who are searching for the "top to their pot." Keep the faith. Dreams come true!

Contents

Foreword, by Victoria Moran ix

Acknowledgments xiii

Introduction xv

CHAPTER 1: The Law of Attraction:
An Overview 1

CHAPTER 2: Identifying Your
"Don't Wants" and "Do Wants" 7

CHAPTER 3: Getting
into Your "Feeling Place" 21

CHAPTER 4: Keeping the Buzz Going 27

CHAPTER 5: Stop Searching
and Start Attracting 33

CHAPTER 6: Fuel It with Passion 41

CHAPTER 7: Let the Love Begin 49

CHAPTER 8: Relating for the
Right Reasons 59

CHAPTER 9: Improving Your
   Capacity to Love 67

CHAPTER 10: How Attractive a
   Soul Mate Are You? 77

CHAPTER 11: Order Up! 89

CHAPTER 12: Nearly "The One" 105

CHAPTER 13: Soul Mates 119

CHAPTER 14: Enjoy the Ride! 127

CHAPTER 15: Ask Marla: Dating Q&A's 131

Appendix A: Affirmations 163

Appendix B: How a Matchmaking Service
   Can Help You Find Your Soul Mate 169

Foreword

by Victoria Moran

The country-music lyric says that you're "lookin' for love
in all the wrong places." Matchmaker and wise woman
Marla Martenson attests that it's more a matter of looking
for it in all the wrong ways. In this bright, no-nonsense
book, she shows any willing single how to both employ a
different strategy and adopt a different mindset in the quest
to find the perfect person.

This is not a slam-dunk. You have to keep your wits
about you. For instance, Martenson is quick to assert that
looking for the *perfect* person is a great way to end up with
nobody, but, in a seeming paradox, you must refuse to settle for less than you deserve. How is a regular single person, weary of the bars and speed-dating and waiting for the
phone to ring, supposed to develop this level of discern-
ment? Are you expected to have some kind of spiritual experience? Bingo!

In *Excuse Me, Your Soul Mate Is Waiting*, Martenson
admirably follows the tradition of Excuse Me series developer Lynn Grabhorn. In similar fashion, Martenson applies
the spiritual, and yet infinitely practical, principle of the Law
of Attraction to rock-solid, day-today life—in this case the
world of dating and discovering the one person you want to
be with for keeps.

This is such a needed concept in our complexity-ridden day and age. We no longer reach maturity, court one or two lads or lasses, and get respectfully hitched before things go too far. The Jane Austen image of a young woman sitting on the veranda awaiting the gentleman who's coming to call is long gone, and even the dating practices of recent times— "I'll fix you up with my brother-in-law"—are history. We're living in a climate in which multiple marriages and blended families are commonplace, and in which most people bring to even first marriages the baggage of previous relationships and great expectations for "The One." In addition, many of us are in the Masters Division of the dating game—in our thirties, forties, fifties, sixties—and all of us are busy with work and other commitments. Even with singles' groups, dating services, and the incredible networking potential of the Web, we need something more. We need the Law of Attraction.

I know this approach works because it worked for me. I'd been single for nine years and was embarrassingly desperate to find the right person. One day, as I sat in my breakfast room, it hit me: "My life is really pretty awesome. I have a terrific daughter. I get to write books for a living. I own my house and, although it's not my dream house, it's mine. I really am okay." I hadn't heard of the Law of Attraction then, but I was inadvertently practicing it by letting go of the desperation and focusing on all that was wonderful in my single life. Two days later I met a fascinating gentleman in a bagel shop. We recently celebrated our tenth anniversary.

In this highly readable book, Martenson shares other happy stories—including her own: she is an expert who walks her talk. *Excuse Me, Your Soul Mate Is Waiting* also provides immediately usable, down-to-earth tips, and easy-to-implement ways to put the Law of Attraction to work for you—in the dating and relationship arena and also in your life as a whole. After all, it's your life—your character, your personality, your passions, and your charisma—that will let your soul mate know you're here. And once you've found each other, it's those qualities in the two of you that can, even in our difficult and uncertain times, make "happily ever after" a part of your fairy tale.

—Victoria Moran (www.victoriamoran.com),
motivational speaker, spiritual-life coach,
and author of *Creating a Charmed Life*

Acknowledgments

Writing this book has been an adventure, and for that I'd like to thank some very special people. First, to all the wonderful people at Hampton Roads Publishing, especially Jack Jennings and his talented staff, Jane Hagaman, Tania Seymour, Sara Sgarlat, and especially to Susan Heim and others who helped "love" this book into being! Also, a very special thank-you to Bettie Youngs, without whom this book would not have been possible. She has been my friend, my mentor, and a great inspiration, and I have learned so much from her. She is like an angel in my life.

Thanks to Bill Gladstone, my agent, for believing in my idea and taking a chance on me! Thank you to my beloved mother, Donna Reed, for bragging about me to all of her friends. To my loving husband, Adolfo Bringas, for being my soul mate, for telling me to keep writing, and for keeping me on track when I wanted to do a dozen other things at the same time. Thanks to Rouben Terzian for telling me, "You can do it." And to Daphne, who will always be in my heart. Even though she's in Heaven, I can feel her energy shining through.

Introduction

It's amazing! Whether you know it or not, you just attracted this book into your life! Think of the many books out there on the subject of dating, relationships, and how to find that special someone. Out of all these books, you picked this one. Maybe you were attracted to the title. Maybe you are familiar with Lynn Grabhorn's book, *Excuse Me, Your Life Is Waiting,* which talks about Law of Attraction principles. Or maybe a friend gave you this book as a gift, or you heard someone talking about it. However it came into your possession, it was meant to be. There are no coincidences. In her book, Lynn showed us that we have the ability to create our own reality—to understand how our feelings attract everything we have and want into our life.

I am living proof of the power of the Law of Attraction. For instance, from an early age, I wanted to be an actress and do television commercials. I used to sing all the jingles and act out the commercials in front of the bathroom mirror. But I was often told negative things like:

♥ It's an impossible business to "break into."

♥ Other people may be successful, but you can only get to a certain level.

♥ The odds are against you, so maybe you shouldn't try so hard.

At age eighteen, when I first told my grandmother that I was moving to Los Angeles to become an actress, she laughed and told me "Oh, Marla, why even try? You have a one-in-a-million chance!" She said a similar thing to another teenage family member who wanted to be a professional singer. "That will never happen . . . she can never do that!" These are very dangerous words because they permeate right into a person's being, into the subconscious. Luckily, I don't listen to limiting ideas, and I can be very persistent when I want to do something. I went ahead and moved to L.A., booked a national commercial for Chevrolet within six months, and went on to do many more.

Have you ever had people try to limit your dreams like my grandmother did? Have you ever wanted to reply, as I did, "But why not? Why can't we become or do whatever we set out to? Why should fabulous happenings only be reserved for other people?" Well, the truth is, they're not. When I was twenty-one years old and working in a restaurant in Hollywood, I overheard one of the hostesses tell a customer, "Yes, I am working here part-time, but I really am an actress." She landed a role on a soap opera within a month! She didn't even have an agent when she said those words. She had just arrived in Los Angeles from some dinky town when a friend introduced her to his agent. The next day, she was sent on an audition, and she got the role. It changed her whole life. She felt and believed that she was not a hostess in a restaurant, but the actress she already was.

Her story is similar to the way I attracted a publisher for this book! About three years ago, I decided that I wanted to write a dating book. There are so many single people looking for the love of their lives, but I knew they were making a lot of mistakes in the dating arena. As a professional matchmaker, I realized I had a lot to say that could help people. I felt passionate and excited to share that knowledge with others. Still, I worried that there were already too many dating books saturating the market. But instead of letting that fear and worry stop me, I affirmed that I had my own style, experience, and humor to offer. Feeling confident in this, I went ahead and wrote a book.

Of course, getting a book published isn't always easy. At the same time that my agent was shopping my book around for a publisher, the book *He's Just Not That into You* came out. Everyone was talking about and buying that book, making it difficult to get a publisher interested in mine. In the meantime, a co-worker gave me a copy of *Excuse Me, Your Life Is Waiting* as a gift. I read the book and just loved it. It became my "bible," and I read and reread it many times. Practicing the techniques, I decided to start my morning walk by affirming and feeling that I was already a professional writer with my writing in demand. I visualized my book already in the stores! Then I let it go. I didn't try to force it. I just used the Law of Attraction techniques, believed my book would get published, and kept writing.

Soon thereafter, I went to a women's conference hosted by a writer friend, and her publisher got up to speak. One of his books happened to be *Excuse Me, Your Life Is Waiting*. I was blown away! Afterward, I approached him and told him with enthusiasm how much I loved that book and how it had become my "bible." He said that they were doing a new series of *Excuse Me* books, and I might be the perfect person to write one on relationships. Magic! The Law of Attraction had worked. Though it has taken a couple of years (as is typical of the publishing business), there is no doubt in my mind that I *felt* and created this opportunity into my life. There are no coincidences. I proved that I really am co-creator with the universe. My dream was coming true. I turned everything around once I changed my thinking and the way I was vibrating. And now I want to make your dreams come true, too!

In this book, you will learn how you can use the same principles to attract your soul mate so the two of you can co-create a new relationship. You will feel in control and powerful as you magnetize and energize your feelings to attract this person to you. And with the practical dating advice and strategies I provide, there's a very good chance that this person will want to stick around.

In Los Angeles, we have a saying: "Everyone's looking for the BBD (bigger, better deal)!" But with my help, you will get a lot more than this. You will learn how to get started on your BBL—your biggest, best life! As you live this life, you will become an attractive and dynamic individual, making you the best deal for that special someone who is meant for you. What do I mean by "attractive and dynamic"? Your personality and soul will shine through, your self-confidence will be up, and you will just sparkle, which can come through physically as well as in the form of positive energy. When we feel dynamic, powerful, and special, it comes through in all aspects of our life.

So get ready to break what Lynn Grabhorn called the "want barrier." Prepare yourself to crash through "a lifetime of programmed deprivation" and find fulfillment. Lynn advises that this "can be a bit scary, primarily because it means changing. But crash we must if we are to become creators by intent instead of creators by accident." What will happen as you break through? You will be in the perfect place to co-create a wonderful new relationship!

CHAPTER 1

The Law of Attraction

an overview

If you are already a fan of *Excuse Me, Your Life Is Waiting* or any of the other books in the *Excuse Me* series, you know about the Law of Attraction. You know that what we think, and especially what we "feel," can manifest what we want into our lives. Learning to consciously use the Law of Attraction is important. And as *Excuse Me, Your Life Is Waiting* first revealed, there are four fundamental steps to using the Law of Attraction well so you can co-create anything that you want into your life. The steps are:

1. Identify what you *don't* want.

2. Then identify what you *do* want.

3. Get into the "feeling place" of what you want.

4. Expect, listen, and allow it to happen.

That's all there is to it. I'll explain more about these steps later, but know now that as you get into the habit of applying these steps in your everyday life, you will notice things change for the better in every area, not just in your relationships. Your bank account won't be as empty, you will have more energy, and your doubts and fears will slowly (or even quickly) melt away. You will feel more in control of your life. You will no longer have that "victim mentality," feeling buffeted around by circumstances that seem out of your control. Especially when it comes to relationships, too many people end up feeling "used" or "victimized" by the opposite sex.

Last year, I was at a girlfriend's house. I hadn't seen her in about three years, though we kept in touch by e-mail through which she frequently told me "how bad things are." As we made some dinner, and then sat down and talked, she seemed extremely bitter. Now in her forties, she lamented over how much time she had wasted choosing to be with the "wrong men" for the past fifteen years. But instead of taking responsibility for her choices, she talked as if she was a "victim" of these men whom she felt had stolen her youth. She explained that in future relationships, she would "use" the men instead to get back at them for all they had done to her.

Can you imagine? Instead of using her creative energy and the Law of Attraction to find a really great guy, my friend was now setting up a reality of becoming a user in a world of users! I have since chosen to let my relationship with her go. I now make it a habit to have only positive, high-frequency friends in my life! That's how the Law of Attraction works. What we believe, think, and feel are what we tend to manifest or create! People who use the Law of Attraction understand this—there is no such thing as a victim. Yes, events may happen, but we victimize ourselves when we don't learn anything from these events. On the other hand, we can decide to grow from our experiences and manifest our BBL—our bigger, better life! Your choice!

VICTIMS NO MORE!

As I said, it's easy to blame others for what happens in our lives—lousy circumstances, bad luck, inconsiderate people, a broken mirror, or a black cat walking under a ladder. We all use cop-out phrases like, "It's just my luck," "Good things never happen to me," "I'm not smart enough," or "I'll never be successful." And what happens when we say these things? They become reality! Our beliefs become real life (see exercise on the next page). So, if you want to have "good luck," to be smart and successful, it's time to break this rotten habit right here and now. Decide to no longer believe and live by the perception that outer circumstances control your life. Throw out notions that bad luck or karma from another lifetime has the power to stop you from manifesting what you want. Permanently move out of the neighborhoods of fear, negativity, and lack. Why live in those dumpy towns anymore? Choose instead to raise your energy and vibrations. Couple these with positive affirmations, and you will be far more likely to attract to yourself a terrific life.

You are not a victim! You were born into this life to experience joy and prosperity. You are here to thrive in light and love, and have wonderful and healthy relationships. You deserve it. You deserve to have all of your desires realized. And this book will show you how to create whatever you want, whether it's a peaceful relationship or a new pair of shoes. As you will learn, it begins with having positive thoughts. But these won't make a bit of difference unless you combine them with lifting your vibration so it can

SOUL MATE ASSIGNMENT

What "Cop-Out Phrases" Do You Use When Things Go Wrong?

magnetically pull those wants into your life. You have to *feel* yourself having what you want.

How do you get the right kind of magnetic vibration? Understand, first of all, that we are made of energy. I know that we look like we are a solid mass walking around on this Earth, but we are actually energy that is vibrating. When we have negative thoughts, we tend to hook them up with negative feelings. These cause us to vibrate at a low frequency. In contrast, when we have positive thoughts, we vibrate at a higher frequency. And when we couple positive thoughts with good feelings, we vibrate at a level that can pull some positive experiences into our lives!

That is why I want you to learn to distinguish good feelings from bad feelings. When you get this down, your life will get moving. You'll be able to create anything that you darn well please! Bad feelings are fear based. Fear-based thoughts vibrate at an extremely low frequency. They keep your good from you. And they attract yucky stuff into your life, making sure that you get more of the same. Bad feelings include anger, resentment, jealousy, worry, and doubt. Good feelings include enthusiasm, love, joy, excitement, appreciation, delight, and gratitude. These vibrate at a high frequency and pull the good stuff to you! That is why you want to learn how to stay within the vibration of good feelings as much as you can.

GETTING STARTED

And here's some more exciting news. You are not alone in your quest to attract and maintain good vibes. You have a creation partner. I like to call it God, but you can call it whatever you please: Higher Self, Inner Being, Spiritual Guide, Intuition, or even Gertrude! It doesn't matter what you call it, but it's right there with you co-creating. Isn't that fantastic? And God put you on this Earth so you can optimize it. He wants you to live up to your full potential and not dwell on all the things that you feel are missing from your life, including a wonderful relationship. So, let's get started on the four steps of the Law of Attraction and how you can use them to find your soul mate!

CHAPTER 2

Identifying Your "Don't Wants" and "Do Wants"

Even though I've advised you not to dwell on the things that are missing from your life, go ahead for a moment and think of those things that you don't want when it comes to your next relationship. Yes, indulge in a little pity party because I'm going to show you how to turn your list of "don't wants" into a list of "do wants" that you can manifest in your life. Here's an example in terms of attracting a great relationship into your life.

"Don't Wants"

♥ I don't want to waste my time with losers any longer.

♥ I don't want to be taken advantage of by others.

♥ I don't want to make bad choices anymore.

♥ I don't want to be single.

♥ I don't want to be lied to.

♥ I don't want to be alone anymore on Saturday nights.

Now turn each one of these "don't wants" into a positive affirmation of what you want to have in your life instead.

"Do Wants"

♥ I do want to spend my time with wonderful, interesting people.

♥ I do want to have a mutually respectful relationship.

♥ I do want to make smart choices when dating.

♥ I do want to be in a wonderful relationship with my soul mate.

♥ I do want to have experiences with only honest and forthright people.

♥ I do want to know that I am making a difference in someone's life and that I am loved.

♥ I do want to be in love and have it reciprocated.

WATCH IT!

Now, doesn't it feel great to turn your "don't wants" into positive affirmations instead? As I mentioned previously, you must be careful to avoid concentrating too much on what you *don't* want. Use an understanding of what you don't want to help you clarify what you do want, but be careful. Sometimes what you want and don't want can get confused.

Just wanting something isn't going to bring it to you if you continue to obsess on *not* having it at the same time. This only feeds the experience of not having, and these negative emotions repel what you are trying to attract. So, instead of focusing on your feeling of "I don't want to be single any longer" or "I don't want to date unavailable men," change it to "I want to be in a loving relationship with someone who is available and happy to be with me." Why? If you only focus on what you don't want, your constant attention on it will make it bigger. Even more tricky is when it looks like you are saying you want something, but in reality you are emphasizing the negative aspects of what you don't want. For example:

"I want out of this depressing, unhappy, and unfulfilling relationship."
"I want to get out of debt."
"I want to get out of this poor-paying job that isn't satisfying me emotionally and creatively."

Where is the focus? In each of those examples, it's on what you don't want. If you are giving passionate attention and thought to something you truly do not want, even when it's phrased as a want, it will eventually backfire on you. Obviously, you can't scrutinize every thought you have to see if it's a "do want" or a "don't want." Your head would explode! But this is where your *feelings* come in. Pay attention to how getting what you want makes you feel. If what you are thinking about makes you feel all warm and fuzzy and happy as a clam, you are into a "do want." If you feel like a dark cloud is over your head, you're into a "don't want."

As soon as you recognize that you are focusing on a

pesky "don't want," quickly focus on what you do want, or find something else to think about that will get you feeling even a little bit better. Switch your thoughts to your cute little dog, the massage you have scheduled, that bottle of wine you will be enjoying later with the girls, that cute guy who works down the hall. Anything at all! And make sure that you stay in that place until you begin to feel your mood change and your vibrations are up. The longer and more often you can stay in a higher frequency, the quicker your unwanted condition will begin to dissipate.

WHAT DO MEN AND WOMEN REALLY WANT IN A SOUL MATE?

So, have you identified what you don't want and do want in a soul mate? If you're having trouble identifying your "do wants," it may be helpful to know some of the feedback I often get as a matchmaker in terms of what people want to have in a future partner. Here are the comments I hear most often.

"Don't Wants"

A partner who "jumps the gun" on a relationship. If your boyfriend or girlfriend proclaimed undying love for you on the first date, chances are this person is not right for you. This isn't flattering; it's creepy. If this person thinks he "knows" you after just a few hours, or even just a few dates, then he's not interested in the real you. He's just interested in having *somebody*. This person might turn out to be a stalker or worse. You're better off alone than with someone who wants to be intimate too soon.

A partner who's only looking for someone who looks

like a model. I know that we all have our "dream man" or "perfect woman" pictured in our head. "He must be over six feet five and have a full head of hair." "She must weigh 110 pounds and have a 36D chest." But if "someone who looks like a model" is your criterion for a soul mate, I have news for you: you're not likely to find the love of your life! And, conversely, do you really want to be with someone who finds you sexy but could care less about the person inside? Looks are fleeting. Seek a soul mate who is beautiful under the skin. You never know what package your soul mate is going to arrive in. Be flexible, and you just might be pleasantly surprised.

A partner I'd be ashamed to take home to my family. If someone is truly your soul mate, that person is going to be around for a long time. Presumably, you want to be with someone who would fit in well with your family and friends . . . someone you'd be proud to take home to Mom and Dad. Don't date a man who wants you to dress like a porn star. He's not seeing you as "wife material" or the mother of his future children. And guys, if you're truly looking for your soul mate, don't date someone you'd be ashamed to bring home to your parents.

A partner who's inconsiderate of others. A person who treats other people poorly, such as waiters and service people, has a poor character. Chances are you will be treated just as badly down the road. Judge a potential partner by how that person treats others. Never settle for someone who's rude or inconsiderate of others' feelings.

A partner who sees me as a sperm bank or a uterus. If you are desperate to have a baby—and, yes, this applies to some men, too—you can't let this affect your search for a partner. Don't settle for someone who's less than a soul mate just because your biological clock is ticking. And if your potential mate brings up the subject of having children with you before you've even had your second date, be wary of being used as a sperm bank or baby carrier.

A partner with bad manners or hygiene. A true soul mate will have your feelings in mind and won't offend you with bad manners or poor hygiene. If he spends every meal on his cell phone, avoiding conversation with you, get rid of him. (If he's a doctor or a single parent and gets an emergency call, give him some slack, of course!) If your potential soul mate always meets you in a T-shirt and flip-flops, and doesn't bother to brush her teeth, then she doesn't care about your feelings. If he burps and farts at the dinner table, and picks his teeth with a matchbook, he's not for you. True soul mates show their "best side," even beyond the first few dates.

A partner who sees me as a piggybank. Does your partner value you only for what you are willing or able to provide monetarily? Does your girlfriend sound like Vanessa, a beautiful woman who uses my agency to get dates? Every single man who gave us feedback about how his date went with Vanessa said the same thing: "She sure is high-maintenance!" Evidently, Vanessa barely has her back side in the chair before she explains to her date that she only flies first-class, loves diamonds, would love to stop working and just lie on the beach with a piña colada all day, and wouldn't consider getting engaged unless she had a ten-carat yellow diamond with baguettes on either side from Harry Winston! She may be the most beautiful woman on the planet, but if you're looking for a true partner, find someone who wants you for yourself, not for what you have in the bank.

A partner who's "full of self." Self-confidence is attractive; boastfulness is not. Men who brag about how much money they make, their six-pack abs, or their brand-new Ferrari aren't soul mate material. This "macho talk" means he's more interested in himself than in you. And it works both ways. Men are turned off by women who are always talking about their looks, their taste for expensive jewelry, or their manicures. Look for a partner who's modest about appearance and accomplishments.

A partner who's "high-maintenance" or needy. Never settle for a partner who relies solely on you for entertainment. Attractive soul mates are independent, not joined to partners at the hip, with their own interests. When I ask my male clients if they care what kind of job a woman has, 95 percent of the time they will answer, "I don't care what she does as long as she *has* a job and it is something that she enjoys or is passionate about." He doesn't want the pressure of knowing that she is just waiting for him to finish work or whatever he is doing so he can get home to entertain her. A certain degree of independence makes for a balanced and healthy relationship.

A partner who talks about the ex all the time. It is a real turnoff to both men and women to hear stories or complaints about the ex. You want to become involved with someone who is over the past and ready for a new relationship. I get feedback so often from both men and women about their dates going on and on about their ex. And often it is extremely negative. Put the past in the past, and focus on the person in front of you. And find someone who does the same.

"Do Wants"

Now that you know what you should *not* be looking for in a soul mate, it's time to switch gears and consider what you *do* want in a future partner. A person with these quali-ties is definitely soul mate material!

A partner who really listens to me. Listening shows someone is truly interested in you. It's really that simple. Lis-tening indicates respect and appreciation for the other per-son. Many women tell me that the biggest turn-on is a guy who knows how to listen. And, in fact, women say that the number one reason they start seeing someone else, or if they are married, have an extramarital affair, is because the other man was a willing listener (and her guy wasn't!). And, by the way, listening is an active pursuit. Seek out a partner who really hears what you are saying, who asks a question now and again that shows understanding and the desire to hear more.

A partner who's intelligent. We must absolutely keep ourselves abreast of what is going on in the world. I can't tell you how many times a gentleman has mentioned to me that he is looking for a lady who is intelligent and can hold a stimulating conversation. A man wants to know that a woman can hold her own if he takes her to a business affair. And a woman feels more secure when she knows her man is intelligent enough to make his way in the world. You and your partner should be evenly matched when it comes to intelligence. You'll never be bored living with someone who's always learning and discovering!

A partner who cares about personal appearance. When couples get divorced, one of the biggest complaints that men have is that their wives stopped keeping up their appearance. Chances are, if your partner gets sloppy about personal appearance, that sloppiness will show up in other areas of life as well. Look for someone who makes the effort to attract you even after you've been together a long time.

A partner who satisfies me sexually. Sex is extremely

important to a vital relationship. A partner who isn't being satisfied sexually will look elsewhere. Even if you're tired or "not in the mood," make the effort. You'll soon find yourself "getting into it" and won't regret the closeness you'll share with your mate afterward. Seek a soul mate who's compatible with you in bed.

A partner who shares my interests. There is a popular saying that "opposites attract," but it is important to share some interests, especially in areas like recreational and social activities. If he and his friends are big on backyard BBQs or tailgating for sports activities, and you'd rather spend the day at the mall, you're going to grow farther and farther apart when football season rolls around. I'm not saying that you must have everything in common, but your partner and you should at least be willing to compromise. For example, I'm not into sports at all, but I went to the World Cup (soccer) in Germany with my husband in July 2006, and actually cheered for his teams. He was ecstatic! Just the fact that I was willing to spend time with him doing what he likes really won his heart. Look for someone who's willing to do the same for you.

A partner who is romantic and affectionate. One of the ways to feel "emotionally" connected to your lover is through touch. Handholding, for example, makes women feel loved and desired. If you grab your partner's hand on the sidewalk, and he hisses, "No PDA (public displays of affection)!" he's not for you. Of course, you don't need someone who is so affectionate in public that bystanders want to shout, "Get a room!" but little displays of romance—cheek kisses, handholding, or a touch on the small of her back—are important in a relationship.

A partner with a stable career. A successful career means "safety" and "security," especially for women who are

SOUL MATE ASSIGNMENT

Identify Your "Don't Wants" in Attracting Your Soul Mate

_____

_____

_____

_____

_____

_____

_____

_____

_____

_____

_____

_____

_____

SOUL MATE ASSIGNMENT

Identify Your "Do Wants" in Attracting Your Soul Mate

_____

_____

_____

_____

_____

_____

_____

_____

_____

_____

_____

_____

_____

_____

seeking a soul mate. Money means many things to a woman: the luxury of being able to take time away from her own work or career when meeting the demands of raising a family; the security of providing for elderly parents; the security of a comfortable and safe retirement when elderly herself. It is important to be forward-thinking and prepared for the future. Seek out a partner who is financially stable. You don't want to give up your dreams of having a family, a nice home, and the things that go along with having a comfortable lifestyle because you've settled for someone who hasn't quite gotten himself "together" yet.

A partner with a great sense of humor. Spend the rest of your life with someone who makes you laugh! Your soul mate doesn't have to be Robin Williams and put on a stand-up act, but being able to see the funny side of life and not be so serious goes a long way toward future happiness. Seek out someone who will make life's journey a pleasant one. If a partner is always tense and fails to laugh when things go wrong, as they inevitably will, it sucks the joy out of life and destroys the pleasure of being in a relationship.

A partner who does a fair share. Do you want to spend the rest of your life being your partner's maid or butler? Early on in a relationship, you might love doing your man's laundry or washing your girl's car. But if you find yourself doing it all, while you partner expects more and more, the resentment will start to boil and eat away at the relationship. Look for a partner who does a fair share. When Katherine gets home late from the office, exhausted and hungry, she knows she's not going to have to spend another hour preparing dinner for her family. Her husband, Frank, who has a more predictable work schedule, often has dinner cooking in the oven when Katherine walks in the door. Sometimes he's even got a load of laundry running at the same time! Katherine loves that Frank is willing to do his fair share around the house—especially since she has a busy career of her own—and he doesn't refer to household chores as "women's work." Frank's attitude about housework is just one of the qualities that convinced Katherine he was her soul mate.

A partner who has a good attitude. Seek out a partner who has an easygoing attitude. Avoid someone who nags, is inflexible, or is always complaining. If you can never seem to please your partner, no matter how hard you try, you're going to have a miserable existence—and low self-esteem. Find someone who doesn't fill the house with tension and anger, someone who can "go with the flow" when things go wrong. Look for someone who's emotionally mature. If you're always walking on eggshells around your partner, you'll soon be in constant pain.

CHAPTER 3

Getting into Your "Feeling Place"

The universal Law of Attraction is the most powerful force in the universe. Some definitions of this law are:

1. You get what you think about, whether wanted or unwanted.

2. Energy attracts like energy.

3. You are a living magnet.

4. Like attracts like.

Remember, the Law of Attraction tells us that what you think about, you bring about. To every action there is an equal reaction. Thought is important, but here is the key: we need to add *feeling* to our thoughts. As Lynn Grabhorn says so beautifully in her book *Excuse Me, Your Life Is Waiting*: "We create by feeling, not by thought!" I think this is magical!

We have all heard of the power of positive thinking. Well, positive thinking is great, but as I have already shared, it is not enough. We need to add good, delicious, cozy *feelings* to the mix. Then we really have something. That's when everything starts to come together, and your wants and desires are attracted into your life. Now, I am not suggesting that you walk around all day like a goody-two-shoes in a cloud, pretending to be happy even if you just got fired, your cat died, or you lost your favorite pair of earrings. But the fact is, what we send out is what we get back. So, since that is the law, we had better pay attention to what we are thinking about and how that makes us *feel!*

That's why, once you have identified your wants in terms of your next relationship, the third step of the Law of Attraction is to combine those statements with *high-frequency feelings*. Remember, you can't just think positively; you have to *feel* positively! Let yourself experience how *good* it feels to finally be living with the perfect person for you in your life. Visualize yourself getting to know this person, talking to this person, holding hands and being in sync with this person. Have your own little daydream about how you'd feel if you had that person in your life right now. Play that movie script in your head where you and your soul mate walk off into the sunset together. Keep at it until you get what I call a "feel-good buzz" and sustain it for at least fifteen seconds to ensure changes will begin to manifest. Don't you feel great? Here is your soul mate! It feels so good to finally be with this person, just like walking on a cloud. Warm and tingly being-in-love feelings are rushing all over your body! Because of having the right partner in your life, your food tastes better and even the birds sing sweeter. Your whole life is getting lighter, as if nothing bothers you. You are in love!

Now add your specific want right in the middle of that feeling, and notice how it amplifies that buzz in your body. You are vibrating at a very high frequency, and from that place you are now able to pull your desires into your life.

When I first learned how fun and simple it was to do this after I read the book *Excuse Me, Your Life Is Waiting,* I immediately told my girlfriend, Kristina. She loved the book and technique, and quickly recommended it to one of her friends. Kristina e-mails me often to tell me that she is vibrating. And she shares all the wonderful things going on in her life. Her financial planning business is thriving, she just started another business a few weeks ago, and she recently bought a new house! And I am certain that her soul mate is on his way as well!

A quick way to get that buzz really going is to think of something that makes you so happy you could burst. For me, I think of an adorable little kitten in my arms, and I plant a kiss right on its little lips! When I do this I can't help but feel the love bursting from inside of me. I know, you might be thinking, *A kitten's lips? I'd rather kiss George Clooney's lips!* Whatever it is, just find it and go with it. I can also get a good buzz going on my morning walk just looking at the sunny sky and all of the beautiful flowers and homes in my neighborhood. I think about how lucky I am to be alive and healthy, taking this lovely walk and enjoying life. Just think how lucky you are to be able to read this book when there are people who cannot! If you have your health, you have something to vibrate about right there. But it is personal, and you need to come up with your own thoughts and feelings (see exercise on page 25). So have fun with it. Remember, you and God are doing this together, so you can manifest the relationship that will bring you great joy and satisfaction in life.

CREATE YOUR OWN DESTINY

I love what Dr. Michael Beckwith says in the book, *The Secret*: "Creation is always happening. Every time an individual has a thought, or a prolonged chronic way of thinking, they're in the creation process. Something is going to manifest out of those thoughts." So, the way that you can use the Law of Attraction to find the love of your life is the same way that you can use it to attract anything that you desire. We are creators of our universe, and every wish we want to create *will* manifest into our lives . . . and that includes a wonderful soul mate! If you mostly think about how hard relationships are or how you are fed up with dating—and you *feel* terrible about it—then those negative feelings will attract situations that are a lot of work or no romantic opportunities at all. But when you direct your feelings toward what you want, and speak in a language that supports it, you are setting powerful creative energies in motion to pull in that which you desire. It can take a while to get the hang of declaring positive statements rather than negative ones—and generating positive feelings instead of negative ones—but don't give up. Allow the law to work for you. Trust, believe, and know that your soul mate is on the way to you right now!

The Law of Attraction is fun to use because you are always waiting for and expecting your desires to manifest. You are creating your own destiny! And, as Dr. Lisa Love shares in *Beyond the Secret*, while you are waiting for your soul mate to appear, you can always focus on becoming a more soulful person (see exercise on page 26). This helps you attract more soulful people into your life who will help you love and enjoy your life, whether you have that one special person sharing it with you or not!

SOUL MATE ASSIGNMENT

What Thoughts Give You a Buzzzzz?

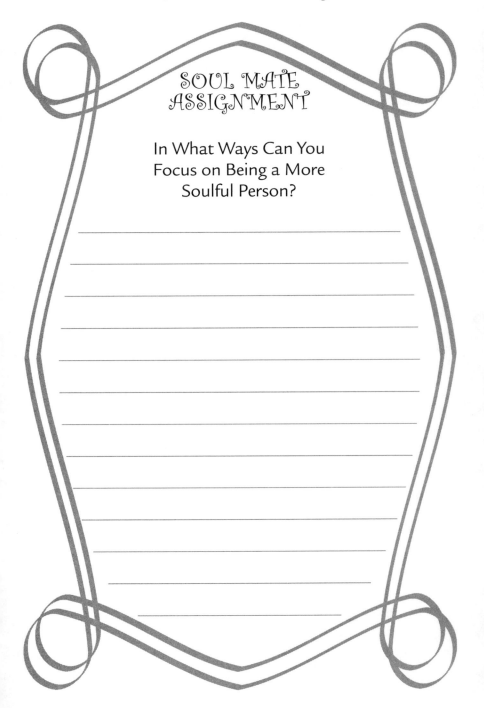

SOUL MATE ASSIGNMENT

In What Ways Can You Focus on Being a More Soulful Person?

_____

_____

_____

_____

_____

_____

_____

_____

_____

_____

_____

_____

_____

_____

CHAPTER 4
Keeping the Buzz Going

Remember that song "Good Vibrations" by The Beach Boys? I can't help but start singing it in my head whenever I remind myself that I need to be sending out "good vibrations." In using the Law of Attraction, you want to get buzzing and send out good vibes to attract your soul mate.

Here are some interesting facts about energy and vibrations: The denser and more negative your thoughts and feelings, the more they will shut out the energy and vibrations of the spiritual realm. They will also prevent you from accessing inspirations from the spiritual realms that will help you improve your life. And they will keep you away from the positive vibrations that help you feel free and light. That is the difference between joy and grief, peace and stress, clarity and frustration. Good vibes attract good situations in your life, while bad vibes attract bad situations. The more joyful, happy, and lighthearted you are, the higher your corresponding overall rate of vibrations will be. The higher your vibrations, the more powerful your attractive powers will be. And the easier it will be to attract a positive person who will be your soul mate!

MAINTAINING GOOD VIBES IN A BAD-VIBE ENVIRONMENT

When I was in junior high school, I wasn't very popular. I had bright red hair and freckles, and I used to get made fun of. I took the bus to school every morning, and kids can be very cruel. Back then, I had never heard of the Law of Attraction, but I started to use it unconsciously. Before I left my house in the morning to catch the bus, I would think good thoughts and raise my vibration. I got a really good buzz on. I flooded my cells with love and with warm and fuzzy thoughts. By the time I got to the bus stop and then onto the bus, the difference in how the other kids treated me was remarkable. Thinking back on it, I don't know how I came up with the idea to do that, but it worked!

Living life with enthusiasm, passion, and excitement, knowing that wonderful things are happening on this planet and that you are so blessed and excited to be a part of it, is really the way to go. But how does one maintain this *vibration* when it seems like the rest of the world is stuck in negativity? We all get bombarded with the news, entertainment shows, gossiping co-workers, stressed-out drivers on the road, unhappy employees at the post office, crabby customers waiting in line at the bank, and it goes on and on.

The good news is that you can *choose* to live from a point of power, a place of peace and joy and relaxation, so that you are vibrating at a higher frequency. Does it really serve you to give someone the finger in traffic, or to get angry because you have to wait ten minutes in line at the post

SOUL MATE ASSIGNMENT

What Situations Put You in a Bad Mood?

_____

_____

_____

_____

_____

_____

_____

_____

_____

_____

_____

_____

_____

_____

office? I have seen customers actually yelling because they have to wait a few minutes. I don't know if it's still the case, but I remember hearing stories about how people in Russia had to stand in line for hours just to get a loaf of bread. We are so lucky to have all of the conveniences that we do. We have almost anything we want at our fingertips, but we have grown accustomed to having everything *right now*, and we don't want to wait for anything anymore. The pressures of modern life constantly threaten to take a toll on our enthusiasm. Much of life is routine, and we can become stagnant if we are not careful. One thing that you need to realize is that when someone is angry, stressed-out, or just plain rude, it has absolutely nothing to do with you. Therefore, no reaction is required of you.

Just the other day, I was driving and a guy was making a left-hand turn in front of me. Even though I had the green light and the right of way, he turned in front of me anyway and shook his fist at me! I could have given him "the bird," but I smiled instead and sent him a blessing. Whatever his issues were, they were not my concern. My concern was keeping my energy and vibration at a high frequency and not letting a stranger's negative energy drag me down.

IS IT COINCIDENCE . . . OR ARE YOU PUTTING OUT GOOD VIBES?

Now, you might be thinking, *Well, how do I keep my frequency up? Do I have to monitor every thought? That sounds impossible and exhausting!* No, you don't have to do that. You are a human being and, of course, there will be times when you feel down. Things happen. I try to keep vibrating at a high level—I say my affirmations and prayers, and recite my script daily (more on this later)—but recently my beloved

SOUL MATE ASSIGNMENT

Has Something Happened
in Your Life That Was Just
Too Powerful to Be Explained
Away by Mere Coincidence?

seventeen-year-old dog Daphne was hospitalized with pneu-
monia. I was feeling down and devastated. I am human,
after all. I thought that this was *it*. I didn't think she would
make it, but sitting in the vet's office waiting, I pulled some
spiritual material out of my purse and started reading it. I
thought about all of the wonderful times I had had with
Daphne, that life is a cycle, and that I had to be strong.

Daphne recovered as much as she could at her age, but
to my horror the bill was $2,200! She had been in the hos-
pital for only two nights! I was frustrated and angry looking
at that bill. I had just paid off all of my credit card debt and
was feeling so fabulous about that, and here I was getting
right back into debt. Then I caught myself. I immediately
changed my tune. I realized that thinking and *feeling* about
what I didn't want (this big bill and credit card debt) would
attract more of the same and make it difficult to pay it off.
So I said a little prayer, giving thanks to the universe that I
had the money to pay this bill and in gratitude that Daphne
was okay. Three days later, I went to my accountant to do
my taxes. Guess how much I was to get back from the government? That's right, $2,200. I paid the bill and all is well.

My point is that you might feel down and frustrated at
times, but it can be turned around with right thinking and
feeling because the positive thoughts and feelings are much
more powerful than the negative ones. We are ultimately
responsible for our own feelings and reactions, and we can
choose peace. There is a sentence in *A Course in Miracles* that
says, "Do you want to be right, or do you want to be happy?"
I don't know about you, but I want to be happy! Think about
that the next time someone cuts you off in traffic.

CHAPTER 5

Stop Searching and Start Attracting

Now that you know the basic techniques for using the Law of Attraction, it's time to focus on step 4—believing in your heart that your soul mate is on the way! Chances are you are like a lot of people and think that you need to work really hard at finding that person. You scan the room when you are out in a club, party, restaurant, the gym, or wherever there might be some eligible men or women. You ask friends if they know of anyone. You put your photo up on various Web sites. You go to mixers and singles parties. Seriously searching for a partner is like having a second job!

If you choose to go to one of the online dating sites, for example, you can spend a lot of time reading the profiles sent to you and weeding out those that might actually have some interest to you. Then you have to write each person. That's most likely followed by a lot of time talking on the phone. Finally, you get excited about someone and decide to meet—only to find out that her online photo is a million years old (or isn't even hers)! Or he forgot to mention that he is not actually divorced yet. Or she neglected to tell you about the three kids she has under the age of five. It's not only time-consuming, but exhausting! I feel worn out just thinking about all the energy I used to put into "looking" and thinking about how I was going to meet Mr. Right.

So I'm about to lift a weight off your shoulders because I am suggesting here and now that you stop searching for your soul mate. That's right, you no longer have to hope he will show up at the next event that you go to. And you don't have to worry anymore if she's in front of you in line at the supermarket. I'm going to show you how to *attract* your soul mate to you instead! When you are doing your inner work, your soul mate will just come to you. It will feel effortless and magical when your soul mate shows up one day on the bus or in spin class. You might be thinking, *Wow, this is too good to be true! Prince Charming is just going to show up on my doorstep?* Well, no, he is not. You still have to be out living your life. You can't cloister yourself in your apartment like a nun or a monk. Go out and have fun. Accept invitations. You need to be out in the world to meet the right person, but the difference is that when you are out doing these things, it is not with the mindset of finding "The One." It is with the mindset of having a great time, learning something new, or having a new experience. That is when you will "magically" meet the right person.

WHY "LOOKING" MAY BE THE EQUIVALENT OF LOSING

Here is an example of how "looking" can get you into trouble. You have probably heard that a bar or a nightclub isn't the best place to meet someone. But a bar or a nightclub could be the wrong place, or the right place, depending on who shows up on any given night. The point I am trying to make is that there is no "right place" or "wrong place." Your success has nothing to do with the place, but rather with the fact that you are "looking." Whenever you go out "looking," whether it's in a bar or a grocery store or a singles mixer, chances are you will become disappointed and discouraged. This "desperately trying to make it happen" thinking, or the "this will be the night that I meet him" approach, actually has the opposite effect.

I have a single girlfriend named Gina. Whenever we go out for a drink, instead of having a relaxing time and enjoying *my* devastatingly fascinating conversation, her head is twisting around like Linda Blair's in *The Exorcist* all night long, trying to see who's there or if anyone new has come in the door. She actually misses the entire evening because she is so engrossed in looking around to see if her soul mate has shown up yet. This is simply no way to live your life, display confidence to the opposite sex, or enjoy the company you are with.

Another friend, Sherina, called me at work one afternoon to tell me there was an international singles mix-and-mingle event going on that evening at a local French restaurant. She wanted to know if I would join her since it might be good for me business-wise. I told her that I was tired, but she convinced me to meet her there. When I arrived, I saw her standing near the bar with a glass of wine in her hand, chatting with a gentleman. I approached and said, "Hello." She immediately glanced around and told me, "Maybe you don't want to stay. There really isn't anything going on here. No one interesting has shown up." I said, "Well, that may be true, but you and I could have a drink together. I haven't seen you in a while." She replied, "Well, we *could*, but you know, I have to mingle." I was flabbergasted! I looked at her and said, "You do that! Go mingle. I'm going home!"

Others can see right through you if you are acting desperate to meet someone. Be a classy person! Prove to the people you meet that you are capable of enjoying your friends and whatever is happening in this instant. Let people see that you are just out living your life with no ulterior motive. Then you may be pleasantly surprised at what happens. Plus, you will be much more likely to meet and attract high-quality people who know how to treat others with kindness and respect because you do.

And the same idea applies if you are using a matchmaking service or doing online dating to meet someone special. You don't need to treat each date with an expectation or desperate wish that this person is "The One." If you go only expecting to meet and enjoy being with a new person, you take the pressure off and avoid disappointment if there is no love connection. Who knows, you could end up making a new friend or business contact, or maybe this guy will turn out to be a good match for one of your girlfriends. Stay cool, be sweet, and have fun!

FEEL THE ENERGY

So, how can you move out of the "looking" mode and shift into the "attracting" mode to find your soul mate? If I had known twenty years ago about using my feelings to attract what I want into my life, I would have saved myself a whole lot of grief! I used to constantly try to "make it happen." There is a song that we sing at my church called "I Release and I Let Go." I love that song, and I find myself singing it throughout the week. The lyrics go like this: "I release and I let go, I let the spirit run my life, and my heart is open wide, yes, I'm only here for God. No more trouble, no more strife, with my faith I see the light, I am free in the spirit, yes, I'm only here for God." It reminds me that I can give up all of my worries, tension, or "obstacles" to the universe. All I have to do is my part by following the basic steps of the Law of Attraction.

♥ Identify what I *don't* want.

♥ Then, identify what I *do* want.

♥ Get into the "feeling place" of what I want.

♥ Expect, listen, and allow it to happen.

As you can see, getting into the "feeling place" is really the "right place" to find your soul mate. Don't look, just *feel*. It's not hard . . . just feel the energy! Energy is creation. With your passionate energy, you are going to attract what you desire. You might be wondering, "Hey, how in the heck am I supposed to feel passionate about something that I don't even have?" Simple: learn to raise your vibration on a daily basis by appreciating what you have. Get into the "passion" zone every day just by feeling gratitude for the wonderful world around you.

On my daily morning walk, I am always amazed at the gorgeous flowers and plants that I see. Where did they come from? How on earth is it possible for a tiny seed to turn into a gorgeous flower with multiple colors? Where did the color come from? Where did the smell come from? Some flowers are purple and feel like velvet. Others are red and feel hard and waxy. What makes one feel like velvet and another waxy? How in the heck did that happen? I look at the hummingbirds, squirrels, the beautiful sky above me, and my energy just rises and bursts out of me. When you eat your favorite food, or hear a piece of beautiful moving music, or someone smiles at you, it puts you right into the passion of life! Focus on what's right in your world instead of on finding Mr. or Ms. Right.

TURN IT ON!

So, you are co-creating with the universe. With your feel-good energy and good positive thoughts, you can accomplish anything. You can bring into fruition your wildest desires. You can attract a soul mate, a new job, a healthy body temple, a new car, or whatever you put your attention on with good, fuzzy, powerful feelings behind the thought. That's why it is important to make sure that you are doing your part by showing up each day, being present and buzzing happily away!

It is so important that you feel good while thinking about attracting your soul mate because feeling good is what goes out as a signal to the universe and starts attracting that which you desire. So, start *feeling* fabulous about your desires! Allow yourself to understand what it would *feel* like to have what you want. Allow yourself to believe that you will have it and that you deserve it. You must visualize the thing that you want, feel in your heart what it will be like to have it, and believe that you will.

No matter what you are doing, you can always turn on some kind of warm fuzzy feeling if you want to. Turn it on as you put on your makeup, clean the cat box, board a plane, or cook dinner. If your desire is to blast out into a new life for yourself, then turn it on anyway and anywhere you can!

SOUL MATE ASSIGNMENT

What Are You Grateful For?
What Makes You Passionate?

_____

_____

_____

_____

_____

_____

_____

_____

_____

_____

_____

_____

_____

_____

CHAPTER 6

Fuel It with Passion

When I interview clients through my matchmaking business, I ask them to give me some words to describe themselves. A word that comes up often is *passionate*. What is passion anyway? The definition of "intense emotion compelling action" really grabs me. When you are truly passionate about something, it will lead to compelling action. *Enthusiasm* is another word that I like to infuse into harnessing the energy of creation. Enthusiasm applies to lively or eager interest in, or admiration for, a proposal, cause, or activity. You want to be enthusiastic about your desires, literally attracting that which you desire with utter enthusiasm. *Zeal* is another word charged with a lot of power. Zeal implies the energetic and unflagging pursuit of an aim or devotion to a cause.

When you can harness the energy of creation with passion, enthusiasm, and zeal, you'll experience every second of every hour of every day to the fullest. The passion will ooze out of you and send those good-feeling vibes right into the universe, pulling in that which you desire! What comes

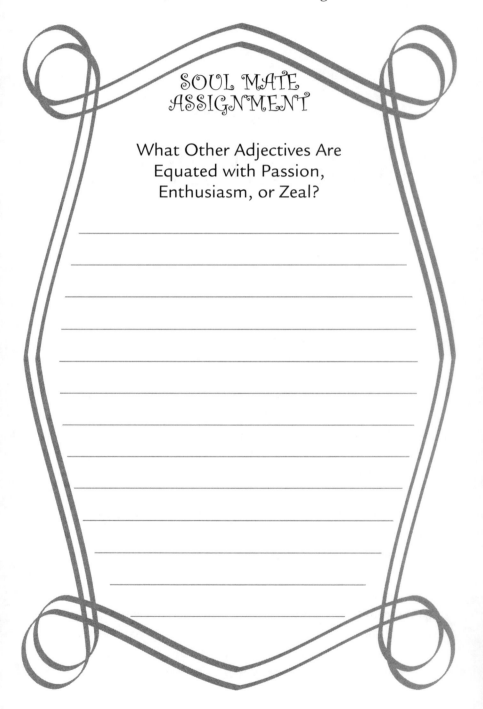

SOUL MATE ASSIGNMENT

What Other Adjectives Are Equated with Passion, Enthusiasm, or Zeal?

_____

_____

_____

_____

_____

_____

_____

_____

_____

_____

_____

_____

to us has nothing to do with what we are doing physically, or how worthy we are, or how good we are; it has only to do with how we are vibrating. Think about how passionate you feel when you are creating a wonderful meal, composing a beautiful piece of music, dancing to your favorite song, painting a picture, or sitting in front of the Eiffel Tower sipping a glass of champagne. People who are involved in charity work, helping others or the environment, have a lot of passion for what they are doing. Making a difference in the world ignites powerful vibrations.

We definitely put the word *passion* in the same category with *romance*. What is it that makes romance so appealing? In our culture, one finds romantic, sexual, passionate love the ultimate ecstasy. The most compelling element of our pursuit of romance is the feeling of falling in love. It is like a drug that we crave. It seems to be a built-in desire for fusion with the other half, a universal, unconscious human need. We crave the passion that comes about as we search for and ultimately come together with our soul mate. But, we can do more than just crave this passion. We can generate this passion and allow it to help draw our soul mate to us.

True, passion can be used in the wrong way. Some women can be "drama queens." At one time, I was one. I just felt so passionate about everything that unimportant things seemed to take too much precedence in my life, like when a guy stopped calling me. I'd get upset even if I knew he was not right for me, but I was so used to the drama that I dwelled in it. Of course, I only attracted more drama into my life! So, passion needs to be directed to the right place.

Using the power of passion in the correct way is key. Using the *feelings* of passion to catapult you into a high vibrational mode is what we are trying to do. When we feel good, we are vibrating faster, the way we were designed to do. Try to get as close as you can to the high vibrations of joy, exhilaration, appreciation, elation, and all of those fabulous sensations that equate to happiness and well-being. It feels good to feel good, doesn't it? When you *feel* good, you are vibrating closer to your real self. That's when you and your nonphysical self are in synch at a marvelous high frequency.

RECIPE FOR ATTRACTING YOUR DESIRES

The recipe for creating anything is really very simple:

Take good or bad feelings, infuse with various degrees of emotion to increase the magnetic power, and out comes what you have attracted, like it or not.

Up until now, the fundamental way that we have sculpted our lives is from the ceaseless attention to all of the things that we don't want, such as not wanting to date guys who aren't serious anymore, or focusing on how all of the "good ones" are taken. It is so important for us to have a broad understanding of what negative emotion is, how to spot it, why we keep having it, and how to turn it around to the positive, because passionate feelings can be used in both positive and negative ways.

I was having dinner with a friend recently, and we were discussing the projects that we were both working on. I was telling her about this book and how excited I was that everything was falling into place. I felt passionate about it, and I was glowing with "good vibrations." She is a struggling screenwriter and has been trying for years to sell a certain

SOUL MATE ASSIGNMENT

Write Your Own Personal Recipe for Attracting Your Soul Mate!

_____

_____

_____

_____

_____

_____

_____

_____

_____

_____

_____

_____

_____

_____

_____

script. She told me how furious she was at a certain man in New York who backed out of a deal. With passion and anger, she ranted on and on about how unbelievable it was that with all of her talent, she was out of work! I started to feel very uncomfortable. I knew that she owned a copy of Lynn's book, *Excuse Me, Your Life Is Waiting,* but I wondered if she had read it. And if she had, she definitely needed to reread it ASAP! This woman has tons of charm, charisma, and talent, but her passionate feelings of blame, bitterness, and anger were literally keeping her desires from her.

So pledge now to put the following ingredients every day into your passion cocktail. Just sprinkle in a dose of positive thoughts about what you want in your life, mix in some really good feelings about it all, then shake it up with good vibrations until it gets nice and fizzy. Drink and enjoy the buzz! I can just see it now. Men and women falling all over you! Why? Because they are magnetically attracted to all the great vibrations you are sending out!

DETACHING FROM THE OUTCOME

To effectively implement step 4 of the Law of Attraction—to expect, listen, and allow your soul mate to come to you—you must train yourself to "detach from the outcome." Simply know that all is well and that your desire is on its way. It is not your job to worry, fret, obsess, or try to make it happen. Now you are self-actualized. Wayne Dyer says that self-actualizers are people who:

1. Are independent of the good opinion of other people.

2. Have no attachment to the outcome. They turn that over to God.

3. Have no investment in power over other people. They are not trying to convince or dominate anyone else with their abilities.

Even though you have put in your "order" for a soul mate to show up, trust the timing of the universe. Don't get in a hurry and force doors to open. If it's not happening yet, it must not be the right time. There is an organizing power behind everything, and when you couple that knowledge and patience with your daily practice of focusing on your wants and getting into that *feeling* place where you are putting out highly charged positive vibrations, then you've got it.

CHAPTER 7

Let the Love Begin

Sooner or later, most of us come to the realization that it's great to have love in our lives. That's probably one of the reasons why you're reading this book! Not only does love make us feel good mentally, but some studies say we are more likely to live longer when we have love in our lives. Love is pretty powerful, isn't it? It's been said that love is the most potent force in the entire world. Is there any energy that has the ability to influence our feelings as mightily as love does? Certainly its supremacy of power is what prompted the great philosopher Teilhard de Chardin to remark: "Someday, after we master the winds, the waves, the tides and gravity, we shall harness the energies of love. Then, for the second time in the history of the world, man will have discovered fire." Imagine love compared to fire!

Bettie Youngs, in her book, *Gifts of the Heart: Stories That Celebrate Life's Defining Moments*, says that

Love is a powerful catalyst for transforming our lives. What greater force for good, what greater depth of emotion exists, what greater gift could one give or receive than love? Some believe that love is our sole reason for being. Our earthly mission is to expand our capacity to love along the way. One of the major tasks we are charged with in our lifetime is to learn to love— to come from our hearts, to lead with our hearts.

Luckily, we all have the ability to bring the transforming power of love into our lives.

That we can give love speaks to the miraculous determination of the human heart to see what it needs time and time again. Even in cases where the heart loses a love or rejects one because it isn't right for us, it begins a new search and quest for love. As that familiar saying goes, love makes the world go round!

Well, no one needs to remind us that love is the essence of life. But just because we all need it doesn't mean we know what we want or what's best for us. Learning what love means to you and to others, and finding the boundaries that make love a healthy two-way street for those involved, are only a few of the lessons we must learn on our journey toward love. This conundrum proves that love cannot only make the world go round, but in some cases it can make your life seem as though it's spinning out of control! Alas, Henry David Thoreau was right when he said, "The heart is forever inexperienced when it comes to matters of love."

LETTING LOVE IN

No worries. I'm here to help! Your world doesn't have to spin out of control in matters of love. You simply need to begin by knowing what love is at a healthy level. It places you in relationships where mutual respect, compassion, honesty, and integrity dominate. Knowing that you deserve this kind of love is important. And wherever you happen to be in your life right now, career-wise, financially, health-wise, or socially, know that you *do* deserve to find the love of your life. As you have probably heard a million times before, life is a journey. Wherever you happen to be on your journey, feel confident that you can be in a wonderful, ful-filling relationship if that is what you desire.

"But, Marla," you might say, "I've tried to feel confident that a wonderful relationship is on its way, but it just doesn't seem to be happening." Okay, it could be that you are try-ing too hard and not allowing it happen. And it could be that you are like a lot of my clients and are bogged down with what I call a heavy-duty case of pesky "shoulds." Do any of these sound familiar?

1. I *should* lose weight before I attract my perfect mate into my life.

2. I *should* become more educated.

3. I *should* be financially stable or have a certain level of income.

4. I *should* get breast implants like all of my girl-friends.

5. I *should* wait until my kids are grown.

A lot of times, the "shoulds" in our lives are just excuses to put things off because we are afraid or not willing to do the work that needs to be done. Fear is one of those feelings that causes a negative vibration and repels what you really want. "But, Marla," you might continue, "it seems like you are not being very practical. If I lose weight, have more money, and so on, won't I be more attractive to a partner? Aren't these good things to do?"

SOUL MATE ASSIGNMENT

What "Shoulds" Are Holding You Back from Finding Your Soul Mate?

_____

_____

_____

_____

_____

_____

_____

_____

_____

_____

_____

_____

_____

_____

Of course they are! "Shoulds" are valid things that you might want to do if they are goals you really want. But those things can be done on your journey in life. You don't need to feel that you need to put anything off just because you are not where you feel that you *should* be. I believe that there is a "top for every pot," and the perfect person for you is not going to mind that you have young children, you didn't finish college, or that you have a size A cup. Your situation can always improve, and you can always improve yourself, but you don't need to worry and stress out about not being in the "perfect" position for having a relationship. Some of your "shoulds" can be fun challenges and goals for yourself to move you along in the direction that you want to go. Just make sure that you always picture yourself in a positive light, and treat yourself with love and kindness.

REPLACE "SHOULDS" WITH GOALS

So, you want to get the "shoulds" out of your head and replace them with goals.

When you write a goal you create a contract with yourself and set in motion a process that helps you carry through. When you think that you *should* do something, it conjures up feelings of guilt and pressure. "Gosh, I should be doing this or that. If I'm not, I'm a loser, or not focused!" When you change your language and mindset to "I have some goals that I am working toward," it puts a positive spin on it and makes life fun and exciting. Goals are good to have because they push us to improve ourselves and strive for a fuller, more juicy life!

Put your "shoulds" and "coulds" away. Goals take persistence, patience, and time, but expect to succeed. You can't always control the wind, but you can control your sails.

SOUL MATE ASSIGNMENT

Write Down Five of Your Goals as a "Contract" with Yourself to Improve Yourself or Your Life

1. _____

_____

2. _____

_____

3. _____

_____

4. _____

_____

5. _____

_____

_____

And don't forget who you really are! You are a miracle and a gift. You are Spirit. You are cut out for whatever you decide you are cut out for. Change your old limiting beliefs about where you should be. The right man or woman for you will love you right where you are!

KEEP THE VALVE OPEN

So, all we have to do is use our energy to our advantage. After all, it is *our* energy. We have control over it, no one else. We can pull a great relationship into our experience with energy. And there is only one energy. Positive and negative energy are all the same, just different ways of vibrating. As we think, we feel. As we feel, we vibrate. And as we vibrate, we attract. You don't have to analyze your past, go into therapy, or revisit bad memories just to learn to distinguish a good feeling from a bad feeling. What seems like "good luck" is really good things pulled into your experience by your positive vibrations.

I can't tell you how many times while going about my everyday business that my mind will start to wander to something negative. Within seconds, I've hit my head on the edge of the cupboard door. Ouch! Negativity can be dangerous! I'm surprised that I'm not brain-damaged from all the times I've hit my head while putting out the wrong energy. The laws of the universe work quickly, as I have been reminded on several occasions.

Lynn speaks in her book *Excuse Me, Your Life Is Waiting* about having an open valve. Having an open valve (feeling good) means positive energy is flowing to us, through us, and from us, and we're creating on purpose. Having a closed valve means we're flowing negative energy, resisting our natural flow, and creating by default. When we are articulating what we want and expect, we must keep our valve open to allow the energy and feelings to flow. When we tune in, turn on, and feel good, we open that magic valve to let our high vibrational flow flood through us. It is also very important to keep our valve open when relating to someone we are in a relationship with or hope to be in a relationship with.

I have a client, James, who was definitely operating with a closed valve. In his late thirties, tall, blond, with boyish good looks, James has done very well financially and is quite wealthy at such a young age. He is quick-witted and outgoing. A cute, fun, girl-next-door type would be fine with him. He has met a couple of dozen ladies through my service, and he told me that he had been on almost a hundred dates through other means such as the Internet. Only a few have led to second dates. Understandably, he is feeling frustrated and negative. But James's frustration and negativity started way before the one hundred mark, and each date he goes on is literally doomed to fail because he is already expecting it to. Remember, like attracts like, and we often attract to ourselves what we expect. Some of the ladies I spoke to about James told me that the conversation over the phone was very uncomfortable, and they did not even want to go out with him. One woman even told me that her date with James was "painful." "That was two hours of my life that I will never get back," she told me.

When I addressed this with him, he told me, "Yeah, when I called the last girl up, I knew that it wasn't going to work out anyway, so I didn't even care." His energy was so negative and low right from the get-go that he did not have a shot in hell of even getting a first date with this lovely lady I had matched him with. He literally just settled in and became comfortable with his negativity. It sort of became his friend. He knew that he could count on things "not working out," so he didn't even make the effort. He just went through the motions of calling the match, but not making sure that he was interesting and upbeat so that the woman was excited about meeting him. Even when he did go on a date, he would sit across from his date at dinner and think, *This will never work out!* And that attitude and energy came right through.

Finally, I called him in for a meeting. I really did not want to see him waste his time and money, and I wanted to turn this around. I started to tell him about Lynn's techniques, and that if he wanted to attract a relationship into his life, he needed to start vibrating at a positive level. I explained that if he was putting out negative vibrations and expecting the worst, that's exactly what would show up in his life. I explained the Law of Attraction techniques I describe in this book and asked him to follow them for a month. He had nothing to lose and everything to gain. He thought I was a bit wacky, but he agreed. Within three weeks, he was happily dating a cute little schoolteacher named Colleen.

CHAPTER 8

Relating for the Right Reasons

When we think about love, our soul mate, settling down and getting married, and so on, we often go back to our childhood thoughts on this subject. These thoughts condition how we think and what we expect our relationships to look like. As a woman I know that even though most women, like men, have careers today and are capable of taking care of themselves, they still like to think that a man (Prince Charming) is going to appear and swoop them up onto his white horse; they will ride off to Dreamland, where they will live happily ever after. Personally, I have worked all of my life. I never expected a man to take care of me financially. But I sure have always relied on the man in my life to help me with my car repairs, computer problems, downloading or uploading photos from my digital camera, and any other technical gadget difficulties. I suppose I have the intelligence to learn how to change spark plugs or figure out why the Internet doesn't work on any given day, but I just love leaning on my man for those things that make me want to run out of the room screaming and tearing out my hair!

The above example is only one of many regarding what kinds of beliefs and expectations you may have regarding what a relationship should look like. And too many people think they should be in a relationship, not because they really want one or are ready for one, but because it's just the thing to do. The pressure to be in a relationship is so automatic at times that we don't even think about it. Do you ever notice that when you are single, friends and family are always asking you, "Are you seeing anyone?" or "How's your love life?" If you say you're not seeing anyone, they all want to fix you up. Your friends all think that you are such a catch, so how can you be single? On the other hand, if you are in a lousy relationship, they want to know, "Why are you with that loser?" The quest to find Mr. or Ms. Right has become so popular that there seem to be a million online dating sites, matchmaking services, books, and talk radio shows on the subject. Everywhere you look, there is some reference to finding the love of your life.

But first, I suggest that you take stock and decide why you want a relationship right now. Do any of these reasons ring true?

- ♥ I am lonely.
- ♥ All of my friends are in a relationship.
- ♥ I can't afford to go to nice restaurants unless a man invites me.
- ♥ I feel like a loser without a woman in my life.
- ♥ My mother keeps asking me when I'm going to get married.
- ♥ My biological clock is ticking.

♥ I want to get over my divorce (or last relation-ship).

♥ I want a man to support me so that I don't have to work anymore.

♥ I want to get even with someone or make someone jealous.

♥ I need a beautiful woman on my arm to feel like a man again.

Many times people just jump right into a relationship or stay in one with the wrong person because they feel that it's better than being alone. Jenny, a twice-divorced mother of two, has a good job and wonderfully supportive girlfriends, but she repeatedly gets into relationships that are not good for her. She is currently in a relationship with a man who beats her and puts her down because "it's better than being alone."

BETTER HEALTHY ALONE
THAN SICK TOGETHER

Watching the news lately, it seems like every day I see a story about someone (usually a woman) who is missing or found dead, killed by an ex-lover or spouse. Even if we are lonely, we need to choose the people we let into our lives carefully.

That's why I am inviting you to really look at whether or not you are ready for a relationship right now. Maybe you just got out of a bad relationship, are recently divorced, or had a death in the family and need to heal. There is noth-ing wrong with being alone and working on yourself to make sure that you are a complete, whole, and healthy per-son who is ready to give your all with the right person. I've

SOUL MATE ASSIGNMENT

List Five Reasons Why You Want to Find Someone

1. _____

_____

2. _____

_____

3. _____

_____

4. _____

_____

5. _____

_____

_____

always liked the saying, "I'd rather be healthy and alone than sick with someone else."

If you agree with any of the following statements, you want to be in a relationship for the right reasons:

♥ I love my life, and I want to share my happiness with someone.

♥ I feel totally ready to find my soul mate and have a healthy relationship.

♥ I have so much to give to the right person.

I remember when I was dating my ex-husband. I was twenty-seven, living alone and struggling financially, and my family lived in another state. We worked together in a French restaurant. He was the sous chef, and I was the cashier. He clearly started dating me because he lived about forty-five minutes away from work and had no car. It cost him a fortune to take a taxi home every night after work. I lived a few blocks from the restaurant, so he started spending the night at my place. Deep down I knew that he was using me, but he was so cute and I was so lonely. He also spoke very little English. (He was French.) Since I spoke French, he relied on me for everything. I felt like his mother. I knew in my heart that the relationship probably wouldn't last a lifetime, but I went ahead and married the guy. He married me out of convenience, making it clear that he wasn't attracted to me in the first place. We stayed together for seven years, but I spent much of that time crying my eyes out.

I was clearly in desperation mode, giving out energy to the universe that I was not good enough to have someone in my life who valued me, loved me, and treated me with respect. Once I started to write a new script for myself and make affirmations that were of a positive nature, things started to turn around. And looking back, I realized why I made the choices I had made and was able to slowly start making better ones.

INTO THE PRESENT

It is important to learn from our past, but not to live there. I think that every one of us has made choices that we wish we hadn't or would have handled differently, and that's okay. I love this quote: "In the spirit world, there is no time." Spiritual teacher Stuart Wilde often says, "We have all the time in the world." Learn from and honor the past, but live in the now and delight in what is to come. If you are reading this book, then you clearly are hoping that your soul mate will be showing up soon, but there is no rush. Value yourself and what you have to offer while putting out the right energy in attracting the right partner.

Here are three things you can do to raise your self-esteem and self-worth:

1. *Have more compassion for yourself.* Know that your past "failures" in relationships are in the past. Everyone makes mistakes or has bad judgment at some time or another. Learn from those times.

2. *Find your personal strengths.* Make a list of all of the things that you love about yourself—those things that make you unique and special, such as your sexy long legs, gorgeous shiny hair, or killer smile. If there is something that you aren't so crazy about, be more accepting or find a way to change it. If you need to lose a few pounds, exercise more. If you hate that mole on your chin, have it removed or learn to love it!

SOUL MATE ASSIGNMENT

Make a List of Things That You Love about Yourself!

_____

_____

_____

_____

_____

_____

_____

_____

_____

_____

_____

_____

_____

_____

_____

3. *Avoid comparing yourself with others.* With all of the images in the media showing us that we should be super skinny and wealthy, sometimes we compare ourselves and feel that we aren't good enough. Keep in mind that those often-air-brushed images are just out there to make money. You are special just the way you are. Enjoy being you!

As you increasingly learn to value and love yourself, you will discover your patience increasing as you wait for your soul mate to find you. And because you will be happy with yourself and your life, this will not be too difficult to do.

CHAPTER 9

Improving Your Capacity to Love

Lani is a divorced woman in her late forties. She looks young, is fit, and has a lovely sense of style. She has three children; two have completed college and the teenager is a junior in high school. She has a nice home, a good job, and many friends. Anyone would think that she has it all, but Lani sees her life as "incomplete" because she is not married. She says she wants to "find someone" and that it's the most important goal in her life. Her friends describe this goal as more like a "mission," saying that Lani calculates pretty much all outings in terms of meeting a man. If she is invited out by girlfriends, she suggests they go to a particular restaurant known for attracting singles. If she's invited to a dinner party, she first asks if "eligible" men will be there. So far, she's found no one "great" to date. Saying that "all the good men are taken," she's moving into the zone of "settling." She recently went back to an old flame who called her. He was an emotionally aloof man who used to call her only when it was convenient for him. Needless to say, she's not happy in this relationship, but she thinks it's better to be with someone than to be alone. Still, while she bides her time with this man, she continues to keep an eye on "the field" for a better "catch." Although she could put him aside and be more open to a healthy and more appropriate relationship, Lani is wasting time with a mismatched partner because she has convinced herself it's "better than nothing." But is it?

While Lani is willing to be with someone even though romance and passion are missing, Roger is not. You might say Roger is "in love with being in love." For Roger, the moment the flames of "bonfire passion" die down, he's off looking for a replacement. In his words, "Passion is what love is about. So the moment romance dies or wears off, I'm gone. As soon as I no longer feel something for the girl, I just move on." In a single year, Roger has had nine different girlfriends. Although he was initially optimistic with each woman that she might be "The One" based on the intensity of his feelings for her, as soon as the initial rush of emotion wore off—as it always does—Roger felt that he wanted "more" and broke it off. Roger's idea of "love" is "passion." There is definitely nothing wrong with wanting passion, but it's not on the Top Ten checklist of what it takes to have a longstanding, mature, or committed love.

RELATING FOR THE WRONG REASONS

Have you ever known someone like Lani or Roger, who go from one relationship to another for all the wrong reasons? Have *you* ever rushed into a new relationship that turned out later to be "bad news" because you didn't want to give up the opportunity to "have someone" after being alone for a while? Have you ever broken up with someone you cared for because you mistook "waning passion" for "dying love"? It happens all the time. When you're beginning a new relationship, it's important to ask yourself, "Am I really ready for love? Or am I just filling an empty place in my heart or simply in love with being in love? What motivation sends me searching for someone?"

Not everyone, of course, is looking for a soul mate or even a long-term relationship. Some people understand that they're fine with being single, and they just want someone to have fun with once in a while or someone "steady" without the obligation to share their home or financial resources. That's okay, too, but be upfront with the person you're dating. If you have absolutely no intention of ever getting married, don't string someone along who's hoping you'll change your mind. Make sure that you and the person you are dating are on the "same page" as far as where you want the relationship to go. If you never want to get married again, say so. If you don't want to have children, admit it. Many people hold off on this "conversation" because they don't want to lose the person they are with. But it's not fair to waste someone's time on a dream that will never come true. You owe it to them to make their own decision on who they want to be with based on their own wants and needs.

DEALING WITH YOUR "EMOTIONAL BAGGAGE"

Some of us know that we want a long-term relationship "someday," but we need to deal with some "emotional baggage" that may have been inflicted on us in our childhoods or our previous relationships. Sherry grew up in a very troubled family. Her father frequently was away for weeks at a time on gambling binges, trying to make enough money to support his family. When Sherry got married right out of high school to escape her troubled home, her new husband constantly belittled her when she expressed her dreams to make something of herself. Sherry left.

Understandably, Sherry had a lot of "baggage" in her life. She had a very difficult time trusting men, and tended to gravitate toward those who didn't treat her well because she felt that was what she "deserved" and thought she couldn't do any better. Chances were great that Sherry would never find the wonderful man of her dreams unless she dealt with her problems. After much counseling, Sherry started to look out for herself better. She realized that she was just fine on her own for now, and that she deserved to wait for the right man to come along, one who would treat her with respect and equality. Sherry is just now starting to date again, but she's being very choosy about the person she goes out with. Now that Sherry has dealt with the "emotional baggage" in her life, she is more likely to find her Prince Charming. If you're like Sherry, always ending up with people who make you unhappy, it may be time to figure out why you keep having relationships like this before you start a new one.

Unhappy childhoods aren't the only events that can leave emotional "scars." Sometimes our previous romantic relationships can affect our readiness for a "worthy" partner. Oftentimes, after a relationship ends, we're tempted to jump into another one to help us forget the breakup or to somehow wreak revenge on our former mate for dumping or hurting us. But these "rebound relationships" are rarely successful. Usually, the new person is chosen in haste, and therefore isn't someone of quality or someone with whom we have a lot in common. Often, the new person realizes that you are only trying to meet your emotional needs, and will high-tail it out

SOUL MATE ASSIGNMENT

What "Emotional Baggage" Are
You Carrying That May Prevent You
from Finding Your Soul Mate?

_____

_____

_____

_____

_____

_____

_____

_____

_____

_____

_____

_____

_____

_____

of the relationship as quickly as possible. You are now forced to deal with a brand-new breakup, as well as the issues that were never resolved from the previous breakup.

If you've just broken up with someone, give it time. Give yourself a chance to get to know "yourself" again. If you're still looking for your former flame's car to pass on the street, if you're waiting for his call, or you still cry when you see another person with bright blue eyes like she had, you're not ready to "move on." You need to make peace with the end of your relationship before you can devote your time and emotions to someone else.

READY TO LOVE AGAIN

During this time of "grieving" your previous relationship, you can also increase your attractive powers to bring about a better relationship next time around. Evaluate the ways you might not have been soulful enough and how you can become more soulful. Did you not spend enough time with your previous love? Did you jump at every opportunity to go out of town on business and your relationship suffered from lack of togetherness? Were you overly critical of your partner's children and drove him away by forcing him to choose between them or you? Maybe you were emotionally distant and neglected to hold your lover's hand or pat her on the back now and then. Did you give up spending time with your friends and now have no one with whom to share your concerns or the issues heavy on your heart?

Remember, the problems in a relationship are usually a two-way street. Most of the time, nobody is really "right" or "wrong" when a relationship ends. Sure, if your partner cheats on you, it's easy to say that he was at fault because he chose someone else. But you also have to ask yourself if you did not meet his emotional needs. Did you create a distance between you so that he had to find intimacy with someone else? Of course, he should have dealt with the problems by working things out with you instead of cheating, but if you can avoid even getting to that point in your next relationship, it will be a happier one for both of you.

So, how "ready" are *you* for love? Are you at the point in your life when you're truly ready for a committed, long-term relationship, or do you need to spend some time alone dealing with some issues in your life? Ask yourself the following questions:

♥ Do I see a pattern in my life of floating from one relationship to another, never really spending time alone to get to know myself?

♥ Do I tend to be attracted to the same kind of person over and over, such as someone who neglects my emotional needs or is never around?

♥ Do I mistrust the opposite sex because of something in my childhood?

♥ Do I still grieve for a past love and hope he will "come to his senses" and want to reunite?

♥ Do I look for my former lover's car on the street or her blonde hair in a crowd of people?

♥ Am I in love with the idea of being in love and can't stand the thought of being by myself?

♥ Do I neglect my friendships or family because I'm so obsessed with finding love?

♥ Am I less than honest about my relationship goals with the people I meet because I don't want them to leave me?

♥ Do I ignore the things that are wrong in my relationships (often called "red flags") because I don't want my lover to break up with me or because I don't want to be left alone?

♥ Do I rely on other people for my own happiness?

♥ Do I feel I still have some "wild oats" to sow and it wouldn't be fair to be with someone who's expecting a long-term commitment?

♥ Does the thought of life, or sex, with only one person for the rest of my life make me cringe?

♥ Do I thrive on the "high" I get at the start of every new relationship?

♥ Does my career or life situation prevent me from devoting myself to someone on a steady basis?

♥ Do I come from a divorced home, or maybe have been divorced myself, and fear making or repeating a "mistake"?

If you find yourself answering "yes" to any of these questions, it's undoubtedly appropriate to take some time for yourself because you're not "ready" for love. Before entering your next relationship, you want to be as "emotionally healthy" as possible. Do what it takes to get to that place: seek counseling, enjoy your friends and family, read self-help books, go on retreats, get back in touch with your spiritual or religious background, pursue a hobby or a new career. Work on yourself. The more healthy *you* are, the more healthy your relationships will be once you are ready to give your *best* self to another person.

SOUL MATE ASSIGNMENT

What Can You Do to Make Yourself More "Emotionally Healthy"?

_____

_____

_____

_____

_____

_____

_____

_____

_____

_____

_____

_____

_____

CHAPTER 10

How Attractive a Soul Mate Are You?

When we are dating, most of us have a mental checklist in our heads about what qualities we want to see in the *other* person. For example, maybe you're tired of struggling to support yourself, so you want someone with a successful career so that you can quit your dead-end job and pursue your life's dream of designing your own jewelry. Or perhaps you are very health-oriented, so it's important to you to be with someone who works out, watches her diet, and is in good shape. It's imperative to know what you're looking for in a potential mate. But at the same time you are assessing others for the qualities you desire, the people that you come into contact with are assessing you to see what you "bring to the table"! Have you considered what *you* might have to offer a potential partner? Do you have the qualities that will be on someone else's "do want" list? We all have our strengths and weaknesses. And, sure, in a perfect world, our partner would accept us exactly as we are. But that's not the way it is. If you want to "up your chances" of finding a partner, you need to take a realistic look at yourself in order to enhance your strengths and minimize your weaknesses. Self-analysis and self-improvement are important tools for making yourself more attractive in others' eyes and hearts.

For example, I have worked with many single women who believe that they are "entitled" to a free ride just because they are attractive. But they are not asking what *they* can give. I actually had a woman e-mail me two pages of her requirements in a man, which included, for instance: "My preference would be to live in Beverly Hills or Malibu, or have a place in both areas. I would love to travel, although my idea of roughing it is staying at the Four Seasons rather than the Peninsula or the Mandarin Oriental. My idea of camping is no blow dryer. I prefer to work at my relationship rather than at a job. I love to travel, and I enjoy flying private, but I am okay with first or business class. Coach won't suffice in air travel or handbags." That was just a snippet . . . there was much more of the same. It was all about what the man was expected to provide for her. With an attitude like that, I was not surprised that, at age forty, she had never been married. Now, don't get me wrong. It's fine to want a man who is successful and has a nice lifestyle. I myself wouldn't pooh-pooh living in a mansion or traveling the world first class, but a man wants to be wanted for who he is, not what he has.

HIGHLIGHTING YOUR STRENGTHS

Of course, I don't mean to suggest that if you've had a string of bad luck in dating that you must be driving dates away with your lousy personality. Usually, incompatibility is a two-way street! Every relationship is different. Judging your own attractiveness to the opposite sex (and I am not just talking about physical attractiveness here) can be an uncomfortable exercise. If you think about your strengths, you may feel like you're bragging about yourself or being conceited. On the other hand, if you consider your faults, it's tough to admit to yourself that you might be able to do things a little better.

First, take a good hard look at what "positives" you bring to the table. Ask yourself the questions below, which might help you to come up with your strengths. You might even want to go beyond this list to come up with some "plusses" of your own! Answer these questions with a "yes" or "no."

_____ Am I open and ready for a new relationship?

_____ Am I fun to be with?

_____ Am I open to new experiences?

_____ Am I a good conversationalist and do I keep up with current events?

_____ Do I keep myself in good shape and looking good for my age?

_____ Am I a good listener?

_____ Am I happy with my career?

_____ Am I financially secure?

_____ Do I have good friends?

_____ Am I generous with my time?

_____ Am I appreciative of what others do for me?

_____ Am I usually positive and in a good mood?

PINPOINTING YOUR WEAKNESSES

Now let's do the same thing for your "minuses." Ask yourself the following questions:

_____ Do I have a bad temper?

_____ Am I overly concerned with what others think?

_____ Do I monopolize conversations?

_____ Do I have an updated appearance?

_____ Am I unhappy in my career?

_____ Am I overly critical of others' performance?

_____ Am I impatient?

_____ Do I engage in a lot of negative talk or gossip?

_____ Am I bitter about a previous relationship?

_____ Am I stuck in my ways and not willing to experience new things?

_____ Am I rigid in my opinions and critical of others' views?

_____ Am I overly sensitive to comments about myself?

THE JOURNEY TO SELF-IMPROVEMENT

Now think about the things that really stood out in your mind when you read through the questions above. Did you seriously think about each question and make an honest assessment of yourself? First of all, if you had quite a few items on your "strengths" list, then congratulations! Remember to show off these wonderful qualities when you're out with someone. But would you be surprised to hear me congratulate you if you had a lot of items on your "weaknesses" list? I want to commend you for admitting to yourself that you need improvement! If you had nothing to put on the "negative" side, then I doubt you really looked at yourself realistically. After all, none of us is perfect. So, ideally, you should have a fair amount of items on both the positive side and the negative side that will give you feedback on how to make your future dates more likely to lead to long-term relationships. If you have self-esteem issues, you may have difficulty getting into a relationship, or at least a healthy one. If you exude self-confidence (but not overconfidence), you will attract the same high-quality people back to you.

Now I encourage you to use the space below to identify your specific strengths and weaknesses. Then for each one, explain how you'll deal with it. For example, if you list, "I have a nice body" as a strength, then you might want to "buy clothes that enhance my figure" to play up this strength. And if you list "I have a dead-end job" as a weakness, you might want to "make an appointment with a career counselor" as your action step to deal with this weakness. Now, it's your turn:

My strengths   **How I'll enhance this strength**

_____   _____

                                              _____

_____   _____

                                              _____

_____   _____

                                              _____

My weaknesses	How I'll overcome this weakness
_____	_____
	_____
_____	_____
	_____
_____	_____
	_____

The goal is always to strive to know and understand yourself. So, don't be afraid to ask for help if you find yourself doubting your ability to change. Take a class; seek counseling; ask a friend for guidance. Do whatever it takes to accentuate the "positives," deal with the "negatives," and make you feel good about yourself! You'll be amazed to find out that when you put your best self out in the world, you will draw the best people back to *you*.

How We See Ourselves

How do you see yourself? Have you ever thought about it? Whether we realize it or not, we are constantly making judgments about ourselves. It could be that you think you need to lose a few pounds, you have too many wrinkles, you aren't smart enough, your credit card debt should be paid off by now, you aren't in the social circle that you would like to be in, and it goes on and on. You know what your problems, challenges, and weak spots are, but others generally do not.

I remember when I was living in Chicago for the first time. I was married, basically unhappily, struggling financially, and going on auditions. I was working in a restaurant, not doing any better than any of the other waiters. We were in the same boat. We were also all about the same age. One day I found out from one of the waitresses that everyone thought that I was a bored, rich housewife, which was why I took a job as a waitress. I was stunned! I guess that I had an air about me that was upper crust, even in a uniform!

Years later when I worked at a dating service in Los Angeles called Great Expectations, clients always assumed that I was the manager or owner. And where I work now, when people meet me outside the office, they assume that I own the company. So, it didn't matter if I was scared, insecure, struggling, or broke. People had a certain opinion of me that often ran counter to my present circumstances. Now, I have also had a couple of experiences where people who first saw me thought I looked like a bitch. Wow! That also stunned me because I am one of the most approachable and friendly people anyone will ever meet. But some people automatically assume that because you are successful, you must not be a very nice person.

Of course, what other people think about you doesn't really matter. What counts is the mindset you create about yourself. I can set my mind and my energy to believe and feel that I am worthy. I can also use it to affirm that I am successful; I am in a loving relationship with my soul mate; I am creative; I am financially abundant; I am working in a career that I love, and so on. So why not accept this invitation to see yourself as all of those things since the universe sees you as all of those things already? Know that you are a perfect creation on this planet and have a right to be here. You have a right to love, abundance, happiness, success, peace, and more. You are worthy of living happily ever after with your soul mate just like in the fairy tales. I want you to visualize it and *feeeel* these things as true until your lips tingle! Feel your way into a fabulous relationship. Feel like you already have everything that you desire and deserve. Have no doubts!

Fabulous No Matter What

So many people wish they were someone else, or that they looked like the latest celebrity or runway model. We have fashion models in our culture literally starving themselves to death. We have women of all ages filling their breasts with sacs of saline just because they think it's the thing to do—even when many men tell them they love their breasts just the way they are.

We Botox every line from our faces because we're afraid we might be mistaken for our real age. But are we just this "container" of skin, muscle and bones, or are we soul, spirit, creativity, light, love, and inspiration? Look to the inside, and you will find everything that you need, everything that you are looking for. Yes, it can be a challenge not to conform, and we all want to look our best. There is nothing wrong with that. But our culture and the media have taken all of this to such an extreme that no one feels good about themselves anymore. And I don't know about you, but I want a man in my life who is going to love me and stand by me when some crows' feet make an appearance, I'm not fitting into a size 2, and I need to touch up those gray hairs a little more often.

I was laughing with my husband the other day at a shoe store. I was trying on a pair of boots and I said, "I used to wear a 7, but now I'm an 8. Everything seems to get a little bigger as we age." Then he said, "Yeah, but then you're gonna shrink!" We don't feel rich enough, thin enough, "with it" enough. Well, I say, enough is enough! The feelings that we need to call forth are the powerful tingly, high-frequency, "up, up, and away" vibes that are going to get you buzzing and feeling great about yourself and your situation because you are going to be pulling in some powerful stuff. So get ready to take control and vibrate your way to success in any area you put your attention on. You have probably heard the saying, "If you don't love yourself, no one else can love you." It is so true. Even when you do attract your soul mate into your life, if your self-esteem is low and you keep putting yourself down, that person probably won't stick around long. Saying daily affirmations is a good way to boost your esteem. You can make up your own or use some of these. (You'll also find more affirmations in appendix A.)

AFFIRMATIONS TO GET YOU BUZZING

♥ Love pours into my life from every corner of the universe. I know that I am loved.

♥ Mistakes don't bother me. If I mess up, I get right back on track. I am gentle with myself.

♥ I am beautiful just the way I am.

♥ I am an intelligent, creative being with lots to give to the planet.

♥ I begin each day with a positive outlook. I intend for good things to happen.

♥ I know that I am fully supported by the universe. I am worthy of all good things just because I am me.

♥ I see the good in others and give other people a chance. Therefore, everyone sees the good in me.

♥ I never give up on things that are important to me. The universe wants me to succeed; I am a success!

♥ I am special and unique. There is no one else like me.

♥ I believe in myself. I am a powerful vibratory being.

It is a great way to start your day with some positive affirmations and visualizations. I like to visualize my day before I get out of bed in the morning. I affirm that the day will go smoothly, that my relationships with my co-workers will be harmonious, and that it will be a wonderful, productive day. We are constantly bombarded with negative junk coming from the television, radio, co-workers, and so on. Starting your day off on a positive note and affirming that you are a positive force in the universe will really make a difference.

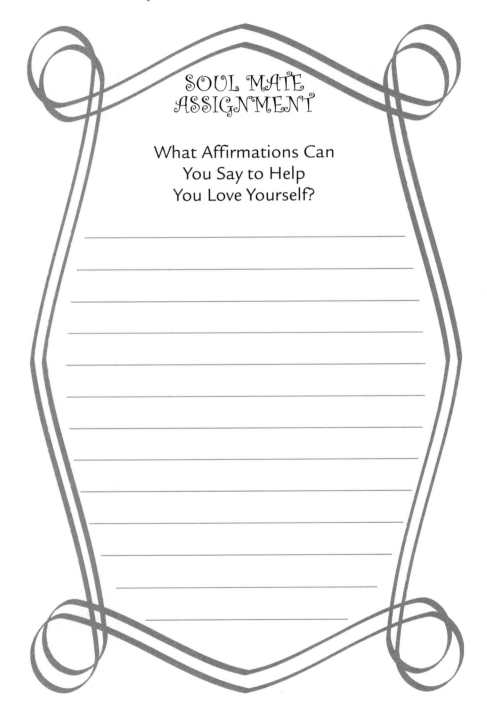

SOUL MATE ASSIGNMENT

What Affirmations Can You Say to Help You Love Yourself?

CHAPTER 11

Order Up!

So far in this book, I have taught you how to identify your "don't wants" and your "do wants," and how to get into the "feeling place" of expecting what you want to happen and then allowing it to come to you in a natural way. I have also encouraged you to understand a little more about what love is and how to know if you're ready for it, and provided suggestions for becoming a more soulful and self-confident person.

You are now ready to increase the power behind your use of the Law of Attraction through writing a script. Writing, or creating, a script is nothing more than making up a wonderful daydream and getting into it emotionally. You are going to make up a fabulous story of the exact situation that you want to be in. Don't make it about what is going to happen in the future; make it about what is happening *now*. For example, you wouldn't say, "Someday I will be working in a job that I love, and I will be making good money." Rather, you say, "I *am* working in a job that I love, making more money than I ever dreamed of."

You must feel passionate and excited about every word that you are writing and speaking. Feel the joy and satisfaction as you get excited about it. Feel as if you are living the fantasy. If there is no passionate feeling behind the script, there will be no change, and you might as well be saying mumbo jumbo. So be sure the higher vibrations coming out of you cancel out the lower vibrations. Now you're really cookin'!

You can either talk your script out or write it down and read it aloud. I like to type my scripts and carry them with me. Then I repeat them a few times throughout the day. I especially like doing it while sitting in the terrible L.A. traffic on my way to work. It spins the frustration into something positive.

Example of a Soul Mate Script: "I am so happy and grateful now that I have a wonderful new soul mate in my life. I love how we look forward to being together each and every day. It is so great that we support each other's passions and careers. I love how we are both so upbeat and have so much fun together. People admire how well-suited we are for each other. We always bring out the best in each other. I love the fact that my partner fulfills me in so many ways and has been such an asset to my life."

LET GO OF THE NEGATIVE

Many of us constantly have a negative script going on in our heads. It's second nature, a habit, like waking up each day, getting dressed, and going to work. We don't even think about it; the negativity just flows. Do any of these statements sound familiar?

♥ "I don't like my job."

♥ "I don't want these bills."

♥ "My boyfriend is so lazy."

♥ "My girlfriend is so self-absorbed."

♥ "I can't get a break."

♥ "I don't want to be overweight."

Unfortunately, that's the type of thing most of us have going on in our heads, or worse, in our conversations with others. In any given lunchroom in a large company, in coffee shops, bars, family functions, and so on, what do you hear? Gossip, negativity, and complaining. It's also what we hear in the media on a daily basis—murders, robberies, wars, kidnappings, and on and on. In terms of relationships, does your current script sound like this? "Why do I never meet the right guy? I always seem to attract the womanizers or guys who treat me badly. All of the good men are taken. I'll never meet the right one." Or, "Why are all the women I'm meeting so shallow and superficial? Can't they see beyond my pocketbook? Aren't there any intelligent, caring, and attractive women out there?"

I once had a dialogue like the one on men above in my head. Consequently, because I kept sending those thoughts out there, I kept getting a slew of unavailable, uninterested men parading through my life. The funny thing is, I knew about affirmations and metaphysics at that time. I was using meditation, affirmations, and feelings to attract modeling jobs and television commercials into my life. It was a fun game. But I had a huge block where relationships were concerned. It was almost like I felt satisfied when each new guy would dump me. See, I expected it, it came to pass, and I was right, by golly! But after a few years of this pattern, I was worn out! I didn't want to be right anymore. I just wanted to be at peace. No more drama, hurtful breakups, or wondering if he was going to call. Once I decided what my "don't wants" were . . .

1. I don't want married men to ask me out anymore.

2. I don't want to go out with men who don't call when they say they will.

3. I don't want to waste my time with men who don't respect me.

4. I don't want to feel that getting into a relationship is top priority.

5. I don't want to get romantically involved with men who don't care about me.

. . . I was able to turn the "don't wants" into "do wants":

1. I do want to only meet men who are available.

2. I do want to only go out with men who are responsible and keep their word.

3. I do want to meet men who respect all women.

4. I do want to put my personal growth and career as top priority in my life right now.

5. I do want to respect myself enough to say no to sexual advances from men with whom I am not in a long-term, committed relationship.

GET INTO THE POSITIVE

Once I got my wants and priorities straight, it was easy and fun to write a powerful and positive script. And you can do the same thing, too. Have fun with it. Make it as elaborate and exciting as you want. The sky is the limit! Your feelings will bring about your desired results. The famous metaphysician and lecturer Florence Scovel Shinn writes in her book *The Game of Life and How to Play It* about digging your ditches and getting ready for that which you desire. For example, if your wish is to attract a husband into your life, get ready for him. She talks about a woman who bought a cozy armchair for her future husband and set an extra place at the table in anticipation of his arrival. And soon she had a husband sitting across from her at the dinner table!

Remember to *feel* the passion behind every word. If you don't feel it, you won't get it. It's the passionate, juicy feelings and emotions behind the words that cause the positive vibrations necessary to bring your desires about. So, feel free to write a masterpiece of a script! Academy Award–winning stuff! This is your life. Your script can be as long as you like, with as many details as you want to include. Actually, the more detailed you get, the more real it becomes to you and the more excited you will start to feel. You can write a new script each day if you like, with more and more fun, juicy details, and see what happens!

Example of a Soul Mate Script: "I am so blessed and grateful that the perfect partner for me is coming my way. We are so well suited for each other. He is attentive and caring and a wonderful communicator. He is supportive of my career and is always there when I need him. We have a fabulous lifestyle and travel to exotic destinations together. I am ready to be present and healthy in this wonderful relationship."

Recently, one of my female clients invited me out to dinner. She had a scarf on her head, and I really liked the way it looked. I like wearing scarves and had not been able to find one that suited me. I asked her where she got hers, and she told me it was actually a man's pocket scarf that she bought in a men's clothing store in Beverly Hills. I decided to go over there and buy one for myself. I went in and saw that it was an extremely upscale shop that celebrities frequent. The British salesman was charming. I told him what I was looking for and he directed me to the scarves. He told me to go ahead and try some on. Meanwhile, some other people came in the shop, and he was helping them. I tried various scarves for about fifteen minutes, and then decided on one. I asked him the price and he said, "Seventy-five dollars."

Darn! I thought to myself. *Seventy-five dollars for a piece of material? I would be dumb to pay that much. I really shouldn't do it.* But looking at myself in the mirror, the scarf looked so stylish and classy. I *felt* rich just wearing it. I decided to buy it and considered it to be my "good-luck scarf." When wearing that scarf, I felt rich and special. I pranced around town in that scarf for the next few days, feeling fabulous. That same week, I booked a voice-over job and a television commercial. I don't even have an agent anymore because I've been working full-time in matchmaking, but two people who knew my work from the past called and hired me on the spot. Then, the same week, I signed up a new client I had recruited and got a thousand-dollar commission. I was *vibrating* at a high frequency. I *felt* successful already. The results were immediate, so I couldn't deny the connection! So, get out a pen and paper and write your script. Feel that you already have that which you desire.

MAKE IT FUN

In *Excuse Me, Your Life Is Waiting*, Lynn talks about something she calls the hundred-dollar trick. It is used for attracting more money into your experience or when you want to improve the way you currently feel about money in order to allow even more to flow into your life.

Here's what you do: put a hundred-dollar bill in your wallet. Keep it with you at all times, and whenever you hold your wallet or purse, remember that your hundred-dollar bill is there. *Feel* pleased that it is there and remind yourself often of the added sense of security that it brings you. As you move throughout your day, take note of the many things that you could purchase with that hundred dollars. Whenever you pass a store or a restaurant, remind yourself that if you wanted to you could purchase something there because you have a hundred dollars in your wallet. By holding the hundred-dollar bill and not spending it right away, you receive the vibrational advantage of it every time you even think about it. If you mentally spent those hundred dollars twenty or thirty times in that day, you will have received the feeling advantage of having spent two or three thousand dollars.

Each time you acknowledge that you have the power right there in your wallet to purchase this or do that, over and over again, you add to your sense of financial well-being so your point of attraction begins to shift. Lynn says that "an old belief or any belief is nothing but a vibrational habit that we respond to like trained seals. So our goal here is to find anything at all to break those old vibrational habit patterns of thought. We've got to give the energy of money oodles of outlets to flow through and to before it can start flowing all around us."

When I read this, I was so excited! What a fun way to attract more money into my life! I have always loved making life and experiences into a game. The more fun I can have playing this game of life, the better! I thought that if this approach could bring more money into my life, then surely it could bring more of anything else as well.

I remember hearing a story about the actor Jim Carrey. Before he was famous, he wrote himself a check for $20 million and kept it in his wallet. A few years later, he was paid $20 million for a movie role. Jim Carrey was practicing the power of attraction, whether he realized it or not.

Donald Trump has made billions using his feelings to attract success into his life. Yes, he started out with some money—his father was a successful real-estate developer—but Donald has taken his life and business to a whole other level with his enthusiasm and his feelings about himself and his business. He feels that he is on top of the world, that he is capable and knowledgeable, and that he deserves the best. Because of that, he attracts more opportunity than ever. It doesn't matter if he is having a bad-hair day or if he has had a couple of divorces or if people bash him in the news. He just feels more determined and excited about what he is doing and it shows.

THE SOUL MATE TRICK

So, what does all this have to do with attracting your soul mate? I suggest you convert the "wallet process" into the "soul mate process" or the "soul mate trick." Write down on a piece of paper all of the qualities you are looking for in the person of your dreams. Make it as detailed as you like. As we discussed earlier, this is your new script. For example, if I were to write one for myself, it would go something like this:

"I am affirming that the right man is on his way to me now. He possesses qualities that I admire. He is caring,

romantic, affectionate, generous, and creative, with a great
sense of humor. He is cultured, well traveled, and bilingual.
He is honest, faithful, cherishes his family, and loves animals, especially dogs."

Put this paper in your wallet or purse. *Feel* that this
powerful statement, this powerful affirmation, is attracting the right partner to you. Be careful not to feel the lack
of this person in your life. Make sure that your feelings
are vibrating the energy that this person is here. Read
through your script several times each day and even say
it out loud. It is important to be very specific and feel the
scenario.

But also look at your expectations while you are in the
dating process. While it would be great to get every detail in
a person that you are hoping for, the reality is you are not
building a mate from scratch in a laboratory like Dr.
Frankenstein. Boy, if I could do that, Donald Trump, move
over for the next billionaire, Marla Martenson! In other
words, you may need to revise or rewrite your script as you
become more soulful and really zero in on the ideal soul
mate for you. The better your script reflects what is best for
you, the more likely it is to come true because you will
know in your heart—you will really *feel*—that this person is
ready for you!

KNOWING WHAT YOU CAN'T LIVE WITHOUT

In an earlier chapter, you identified your "do wants"—
the qualities you really want to find in a soul mate. As you
become more experienced at using the Law of Attraction,
you'll find that you're constantly retooling that list—and
subsequently your script—as you pay more attention to the

qualities that you just can't compromise on when it comes to happily cohabitating with a future partner. Consider some of these potential areas of conflict:

Brains: How intelligent do you want your partner to be? Do you want someone with whom you can have intellectually stimulating conversations, or do you feel threatened by someone who seems to "know it all"?

Status: Is it important that you be from the same social circle? If you lead a life of dinner parties and theater-going, and your partner has never ventured beyond the local Cineplex, you may find that your interests are just too divergent to find common ground.

Religion: If you and your partner are from different religious backgrounds, you may find yourself having conflicts during the holidays, with your families, and in raising children. If you are not very observant, you may be willing to let your partner have the upper hand in deciding religious matters. But if your religion is important to you, think long and hard before hooking up with someone who doesn't share the same views.

Politics: Although Arnold Schwarzenegger and Maria Shriver have managed to maintain an apparently successful marriage despite vastly different political backgrounds, this is certainly an exception to the rule. Your political ideals say a lot about your views on social issues, government regulation, the environment, and so many other things. If your politics don't "mesh," you may find yourself arguing about major life issues.

Culture: Lisa's family is from China. Lisa's fiancé, Anthony, is from a boisterous Italian family. When Lisa and Anthony took both their parents out to dinner, it was disastrous. Lisa's parents were appalled by the way Anthony's parents laughed so loudly in the restaurant and joked

SOUL MATE ASSIGNMENT

Creating Your "Must Have" List

Take the time to make your own "must have" list. I have provided some categories below to get you thinking. Once you've added these to your list of "do wants," you can use them to write your own soul mate script.

Looks: _____

Money: _____

Intelligence: _____

Physical Fitness: _____

Friends or Social Status: _____

Common Interests: _____

Religion: _____

Politics: _____

Lifestyle: _____

Culture: _____

Other: _____

around with the waiter. Anthony's parents found Lisa's parents to be "stuffy" and too "stiff" for their tastes. Lisa and Anthony are always going to be dealing with this "culture clash" at future family gatherings.

Common interests: How important is it to you that your partner and you do everything together? If your boyfriend loves football and you can't stand it, will you start to resent how much time he spends in front of the television during football season?

When considering a long-term relationship, these issues can become critical in determining whether you will succeed in building a lasting partnership. It's important to clarify in your mind what you can really "live with" in a partner whom you hope will be in your life for a very long time. Major differences in these areas can become divisive sources of tension in a relationship. You can prevent this from happening by giving plenty of thought to the qualities you want in your future partner and not compromising by settling for less.

EASY DOES IT!

Up until now, I've been encouraging you to get specific with your intentions, but at the same time it may be advisable to relax your expectations. In my matchmaking service, I have had a number of clients get too picky at times. They've focused too much on their "don't wants," such as refusing to meet women with brown eyes, a B-cup chest, or curly hair, or who are Jewish (even though they themselves are Jewish)! One man would not meet a fabulous woman because her parents were from Mexico. I have had women clients who wouldn't date a man if he didn't own his own home, if he was less than six feet tall, if he'd never been married at forty, or if his hairline was receding.

Humans aren't perfect, and if you "hold out" for "perfection"—if your script is *too* restrictive—you just might want to get real comfy with the fact that you could be alone for a very long time. If I had a magic wand, there would be some things that I would change about my husband. I would love if he were a vegan like me and if he would put down the toilet seat after peeing, among a few other things. And I know there are at least half a dozen things that he would wave his wand over me to change, but we accept each other and the fact that we will always have our differences. The differences are really not important at all. It's all the wonderful, positive things about each other that we appreciate and enjoy, and we have a good laugh about the rest!

As long as the main qualities are there, be open-minded and don't write someone off because of his eye color or hairline. Chemistry is the real key. We see that example in the story of *Beauty and the Beast,* where the beauty sees the beast's inner beauty shining like a star. You might be saying, "Marla, I am sorry, but I just cannot date someone I am not attracted to. Looks are extremely important to me! I'm just not into short guys or blondes!" When I am interviewing a new woman for our service and I ask her what type of look she is interested in, 90 percent of the time she will say, "I have to be attracted to him." Well, I am not suggesting that you date every Tom, Dick, and Harry, or Sue, Jane, or Mary! I'm not going to tell you to date the creature from the black lagoon just because he asks you out! I am simply suggesting that you be a bit open-minded when it comes to eyes or hair color, a few extra pounds, or an inch or two. Try to find all of the wonderful qualities in someone. Let that person's inner light shine through as well.

SOUL MATE ASSIGNMENT

Write Your Script!

_____

_____

_____

_____

_____

_____

_____

_____

_____

_____

_____

_____

_____

_____

So, when writing your script and imagining your perfect mate, know that the universe might have something a bit different in store for you than all of the little details that you imagined, but the universe always has your highest good in mind!

CHAPTER 12
Nearly "The One"

At last, you are attracting a number of soul mate possibilities into your life! You are using the four-step process and other elements of this book, and you might even be attracting to yourself a number of choices. And you may even have found that special someone you hope feels the same way about you. How do you know if you have found the right one? Sometimes we just know it, and it works without a hitch. But sometimes we go through a different process—a series of "near-fits" or "almost-matches"! But that's okay. When this happens, it can be turned around for good. These experiences can help us clarify our "don't wants," so we can turn them into "do wants" and get that much closer to attracting the right person for us the next time around. It also reveals the importance of seeing that someone is the "almost one," instead of the "right one" for you, so you can let people go who are really not meant to be with you in the long run.

AN "ALMOST-MATCH" STORY
Jeanette and Gregory met one evening in a crowded restaurant. They were both out with friends for dinner and

were waiting for an available table. Seated next to each other in the lounge area, they struck up a conversation. Their chemistry was instant, and for the next three years they were virtually inseparable. Nevertheless, there were times when Jeanette would get together with her girlfriends to moan and groan over her conflicted feelings for Gregory. On the one hand, she felt she loved Gregory, but on the other, for some reason, she couldn't see herself spending her future with him.

"Awesome chemistry" aside, Jeanette and Gregory could not have been more different. Jeanette was a professor of graduate school education. Gregory, a cowboy at heart, was a sometimes handyman, picking up odd jobs when he needed the money. When he'd earned enough putting on a porch for someone or repairing a shed here and there, he'd pack up the two horses he'd adopted (on a Bureau of Land Management wild horse roundup) and head for the mountains. He was, as he often said, "working to live, not living to work." In the beginning, Jeanette loved that about him, especially since her lifestyle was more "living to work." She prided herself on working a seventy-hour week and climbed one step higher on the pay scale every year. Her goal was to make full professor within the next two years, and after that to "punch the assistant and then deanship positions." Ultimately, her goal was to one day become university president.

But with Gregory in her life, Jeanette found herself sleeping in the mountains every weekend, under the stars with a cowboy who pitched a tent, started a bonfire, and knew how to cook a mean steak over an open fire. Never an "outdoor girl," Jeanette nonetheless bought some Levi's, as well as her first ever pair of cowboy boots and a cowgirl hat. For the first six months, she loved being with her "rugged he-man" and found the weekend mountain retreats romantic. But she began to miss weekend get-togethers with friends and felt as though she was losing touch with city life altogether. Being away from her home for long weekends also left little time for doing laundry, running errands, and shopping. She found her "to-do" list during the week getting longer and longer, and her friends were becoming a thing of the past.

But Jeanette's problems with Gregory were more than about spending too many nights under the stars and not enough time at home. After many months of "moonlit discussions," she realized that Gregory was living the life of his dreams, so why should he change anything? Jeanette had to admit she was spending time with someone who was never going to fit into her world and, the truth was, she had absolutely no intention of fitting into his. She didn't like "horse life," as she called it, and she knew that to expect anything different from Gregory was not fair to him. But staying in this relationship wasn't fair to her either.

Despite her reservations, Jeanette stayed for two-and-a-half more years! When Gregory gave her an ultimatum to marry him or leave, she finally broke off the relationship. Even though it was Jeanette's decision to leave, it took her heart almost a full year before she felt ready to move on and be willing to love again. Her final assessment: "Gregory and I were so different that it was never going to work out. We each lost four years of valuable time. Given that we each wanted eventually to find someone to marry, we should have broken it off when we knew it wasn't going to work."

Jeanette stayed because of "chemistry" and because "we loved like there was no tomorrow." Okay, so that is tough to walk away from! And sometimes that's enough if both parties agree that marriage is not desirable. But for most people, at least, having the "option" of getting married is what they're after, so prolonging a relationship that isn't going to bring that can be a loss of treasured time.

Are You Hoping Someone Will Change?

Another reason we may stay too long in a relationship is that we hope the person will change. We tell ourselves, "I've found the perfect person for me. If only this person could change this or that, we would be incredible together." Listen up. This is really quite dangerous! You *cannot* change someone. It is very important to realize this. It is so tempting to try to do so when we find someone that seems *so* irresistible. I have heard too many people, especially women, say something like, "He has such potential. I can change him." They hook up with someone who is disrespectful toward others, doesn't like animals, swears a lot, smokes, drinks too much, is into porn, loves heavy metal, hates big cities, is allergic to cats, hunts, watches Monday night football with the guys, uses his treadmill as a clothes hanger, prefers hot dogs to caviar, is a Republican or a Democrat, is a snob, is a gym rat . . . and then thinks she'll be able to change him!

Here's a great tip: don't waste your time attracting *potential*. Spend your energy attracting the person who is already right for you! Find someone who *already* has the qualities that you are looking for in another person. No one wants to be changed or nagged or disapproved of. Yes, once two people are in a committed relationship, there are things that each might have to bend a bit or compromise on to live together harmoniously. (Like I said, I am still trying to convince my husband to put down the toilet seat!) But, in general, you can't change someone, so don't even try! If you don't like the qualities that your partner possesses, either accept them or break up and find a partner who already has those qualities that you are seeking. Stick to your soul mate script and don't deviate from it just because you think you might be able to get somebody to conform to it. You won't!

SOUL MATE ASSIGNMENT

Describe a Time When You Stayed in a Relationship "Too Long"— and for the Wrong Reasons

_____

_____

_____

_____

_____

_____

_____

_____

_____

_____

_____

_____

_____

_____

ARE YOU STAYING FOR THE "PERKS"?

Another reason people stay with someone who isn't totally right is because they convince themselves that "things are good enough—for now." Or perhaps they like the "perks" that come with the relationship, such as "free sex" or a fancy lifestyle (nice restaurants, theater or concert tickets, entry into a more upscale social circle, etc.). And some people stay because they don't want to disrupt their children's lives, or their current situation works well with raising children. But what if you're hoping to find your "beloved"? Can you do that if you're "biding your time" with someone else? This greatly limits your opportunities for finding Mr. or Ms. Right, and it really isn't fair to the person you have no intention of marrying. Sometimes you have to ask yourself some serious questions about what you want. If chemistry is all you have in common with your partner, such as was true for Jeanette and Gregory, is that enough to satisfy you for the rest of your life? Will staying in a "comfortable" relationship make your heart soar even though the partnership is more or less loveless? Let's take a look at Mike and Marie, who got to the point where they had to ask themselves these very questions.

KICKING YOURSELF FOR WASTED YEARS

Mike and Marie, both in their fifties, were both conservation supervisors serving different districts in a large Midwestern city. Over the years, they crossed paths in their work, and they grew to greatly respect and admire each other. One day while standing in a small group of associates, Marie mentioned that she had lost her husband to melanoma. Mike had also lost his spouse years ago. Surprised to learn that each was now single, they talked after their gathering and made plans for dinner. This grew into a steady relationship that Mike described as "comfortable." They shared careers, enjoyed the city, and spent time with friends—but there was no real "spark" between them. They were content, but nothing more.

And then one day, out of the blue after five years of dating, Marie announced to Mike that she had fallen "utterly in love" with someone else and intended to marry him (which she did three months later!). Mike was shocked, but admitted that neither of them had ever been marriage-minded about the other. In fact, they had told each other that neither would probably marry since life was good and comfortable as it was. But while they were saying one thing to each other, deep inside their hearts they both hoped to find the "perfect-for-me" person. Unexpectedly, Marie "stumbled" across the "love of her life" one day.

"I kick myself now," says Mike, "because I want what Marie has—a great love. We both knew it wasn't going to be with each other, but we prolonged the inevitable. It was time I could have better used to find the right person for me, just as Marie now has for herself."

TAKING STOCK: THE SIX-MONTH ASSESSMENT

How can you tell if it's time to break up with your current partner and focus on finding your soul mate? Ask yourself these questions:

1. What's important to me in a relationship? Am I getting these things from the person I'm seeing? Does my partner match the script I've written?

2. Is the person I'm seeing willing to talk about our differences, and, if so, is resolution possible?

3. Have I discussed the really important things about being a couple, such as how to handle finances, insurance policies, children, family, goals, and so on? Are we in agreement?

4. Do I respect this person? Am I proud to introduce this person to my friends and family—or do I avoid it because I know the person is a bit "rough"?

5. Do we have fun together? Do we laugh together and spend time on things that interest both of us?

6. Does this person let me be me . . . or do I find that I'm always adjusting my preferences or behavior to suit the other person?

7. Is my partner considerate of me? Does he ask my opinion before making decisions? Does she do what she pleases and expect me to go along?

8. If I have children, how does this person treat them? Does my partner make an effort to spend time with them and speak respectfully to them? Does my partner get jealous when I spend time with my children?

9. What were the reasons for my partner's previous breakups? For example, if his previous marriage broke up because he traveled a great deal for his job, and he continues to do so, am I prepared to spend a lot of evenings alone when we are married?

10. Can I honestly tell myself that this person is the "love of my life" . . . or am I still keeping an eye on "the field" in case my "true love" is still out there?

You might also want to consider the following:

1. Write a list of your partner's good and bad features. See if the negatives outweigh the positives.

2. Compare the relationship to what you thought a perfect relationship looks like.

3. Ask yourself: Does this person make me happy? Was I happier when I was single? Am I depressed or crying a lot with this person?

4. Would you rather be with someone else?

5. Can you picture yourself with this person for the next few hours? The next few months? The next forty years?

6. Have your good friends been alienated from you since you got involved with this person?

7. Are you constantly looking for excuses not to see this person?

Assessing whether to continue a relationship can be one of the toughest decisions you'll ever make. Sometimes you almost wish your partner would make it easier on you by breaking it off or cheating on you. But most of the time, the decision is not that clear-cut. If things are "okay" or "fine" or "comfortable," it's time to ask yourself what you want from the relationship and whether your partner is providing them. Go back over your list of "do wants" and your script. Don't let yourself be fooled into thinking that if someone is "close enough" to your script that you should "settle." Remember, you deserve to be loved! You deserve to have the love of your life! You can attract your soul mate to you if you keep focused on what you really want, and don't blindly ignore the things you don't. So why waste time? Let the negative relationships that lower your vibrations go. Then tune up with good vibrations to find the person who is really suited for you.

"THE ULTIMATUM"

Although Jeanette and Gregory, as well as Mike and Marie, were pretty much on the same page as far as where their relationships were going (all knew they weren't with "The One"), sometimes a relationship can be a little more lopsided. Often one party wants to get married, but the other isn't interested, isn't sure, or just hasn't come to "that place" yet. This is usually when "The Ultimatum" rears its ugly head. Although it has a "bad rap," it actually serves its purpose. Nobody wants to waste time with someone who doesn't share the same goals. So rather than drag a relationship out for years, hoping that your partner's views on marriage may change (which is rare), it's usually better to have "The Talk" within a more reasonable period of time, say, six months to a year after you start dating.

This is how it works. First, have a talk with yourself. What are your goals for life? Do you really prefer marriage to the freedom of being single? Is your biological clock ticking? Can you see yourself spending the rest of your life with this person? If your answers to these questions indicate that you're not with the right person, it's time to break it off. But what if your answers lead you to believe that you really could be happy married to this person? Then it's time to see if this person feels the same way. How should you go about it?

IT'S TIME FOR "THE TALK"

As I stated before, honesty really is the best policy. In a non-threatening way, tell your partner how you feel. "I've been single for a long time, and I really want the security of a more permanent relationship. I'd like to know if you see us being married within the next year or so." Don't let your partner get away with vague answers or avoid the question. Explain that the truth is very important to you. Perhaps your partner has been thinking about marriage, but just didn't know how or when to bring it up. Or possibly, this person never had any intention of popping the question, in which case you're better off knowing now rather than after spending several years together watching other marriage-minded people pass you by!

Get a "straight" answer. It's true that you might not like what you hear, but in the long run you'll be happy you found out early and didn't waste years with someone who wasn't destined to be your spouse. Stop being content with "comfortable" and start examining your relationship in depth.

How Do I Give the "Heave-Ho" When It's a "No-Go"?

If you do decide to end a relationship with someone, please understand there are ways to approach it and ways not to approach it. Susan, a waitress, was dating a sexy doctor. She was very attracted to him and definitely wanted the relationship to continue. They had been dating for about five months. Even though he had an extremely busy schedule, they managed to see each other regularly and he called often. Then one week, she did not hear from him at all. She found that strange and became worried about him. She figured that he must be in a coma or dead; otherwise, he would have called. She finally dialed his number one evening from work while on her break just to see if he was alive. She was astonished that he answered the phone. She said to him, "Oh good, you're alive. I just wanted to make sure that you were all right. I see that you are, so good-bye!"

He replied, "That's it?"

"Yes," she said. "Obviously you are not interested in talking to me or you would have called!"

"Well," he answered, "I just don't see any future for us."

Dazed by his response, she finally asked, "So, you were just never going to call me again?"

"That's right," he said.

She hung up and ran into the ladies' room in tears.

This is not the way to give someone the "heave-ho" even if you know for sure that it's a definite "no-go"! Everyone has feelings and deserves to be treated with respect. Never leave a breakup phone message or e-mail. This is a cop-out that saves you the hassle of dealing with another person's feelings. Your partner deserves to be told in person. Don't have the good-bye discussion in the middle of a restaurant. Find a quiet place where you both feel comfortable and can talk openly. Explain that you feel you simply are not meant for each other. Don't be accusatory and point out everything that this person ever did wrong. Just explain that you do not feel the same way that you did before. If you focus on how *you* feel, that *you* no longer feel attracted, this is easier for the other person to accept as a reason to break up. If you are honest and thoughtful about the breakup, then you have done both of you a favor. You will both be free to find someone who is the perfect match. Be proud that you followed your inner voice and your gut feelings. Breaking up is never easy, but you'll both recover and move on with your lives.

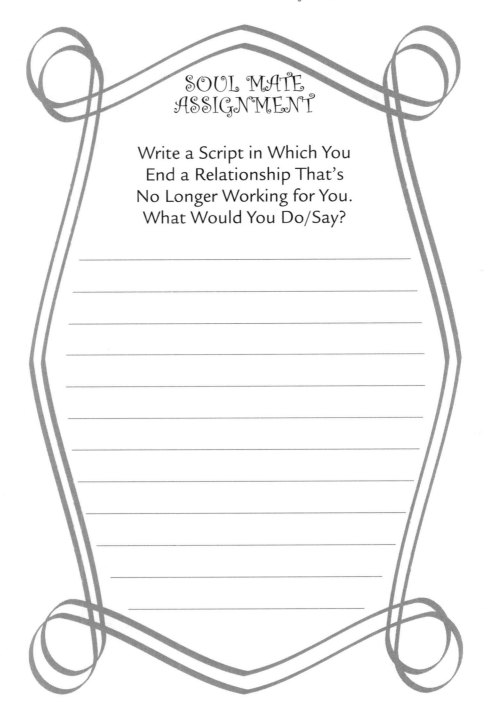

SOUL MATE ASSIGNMENT

Write a Script in Which You
End a Relationship That's
No Longer Working for You.
What Would You Do/Say?

CHAPTER 13
Soul Mates

By this time, I hope you have a great deal of clarity that will help you understand how the Law of Attraction works. Now I would like to share some final insights I have gained from my matchmaking interviews that will help you understand how people finally know if they have found their soul mate.

TIMING IS IMPORTANT

So, you have identified your "don't wants," isolated your "do wants," and written your script. You are vibrating at a high frequency and reciting your script. Excellent! But still, you might be wondering, *Now, where the heck is my soul mate? I'm doing my work, I am vibrating to the point that I think I'll explode, and no one is showing up!* Patience is so important, as well as detaching yourself from the outcome. Do your work and know that the right person is on the way. But it is important to *detach*. The universe is waiting for you to let go.

Many of us don't like to let go and detach from the outcome. If we do that, then there's no drama. We are used to trying to "make it happen." When we do that, at least we can say, "Hey, I tried my best!" The truth is, you don't have to struggle at all. You don't have to make anything happen. You only need to recite your script, believe, feel, and expect. And have some patience. The right person for you might not be living down the street from you. You might live in Atlanta, and he lives in Detroit at the moment. She might be going through a divorce and not ready to meet you yet, or maybe she is taking a break from dating and working on herself.

The universe will take care of it. You will meet at the right time. He might be getting transferred at his job in six months and move to Atlanta. Once her divorce is final, she might run into you at the grocery store. If I had not moved back to Los Angeles because of my father's death, I would not have been in the right place at the right time to meet my husband. Six months prior, he had prayed to God to send him someone special, but I was living in Chicago. Circumstances, although heartbreaking, brought me to Los Angeles, and our energy brought us together. We cannot force things in life. Timing is an absolute. I have lived in three states in this country, and during those specific times, I met certain people with whom I will be friends forever, people whom I couldn't imagine not having in my life. The phrase "being in the right place at the right time" is so true. There are even jobs that I have gotten by "chance," by being in the right place and knowing the right person.

There is a saying in Taoism: "Infinite patience brings immediate results." This is true when we do our inner work. There is no reason to doubt because this is the law of the universe. This is how energy works, plain and simple. If you can learn to let go and to trust, things come much easier

SOUL MATE ASSIGNMENT

Describe a Situation in Your Life in Which the Universe Arranged "Perfect Timing"

_____

_____

_____

_____

_____

_____

_____

_____

_____

_____

_____

_____

than if you fight for it. Surrender control, and you free the universe to bring you whatever you want.

Is He "Not Ready for a Relationship"— or Not Ready for *You*?

Ladies, it might interest you to know that few men who say they are not ready for a relationship really mean it that way. Though it may be hard to accept, if they feed you that line, it really means that they are not fully interested in you! When a guy is interested in you, he will call, no matter how busy he is. He will make sure that he "reserves" you for himself. He will make sure you have plans for the weekend— and the plans are with him. If you've been in a relationship for longer than three months, and have to ask where you stand in the relationship, you might as well sit down because the bad news is coming (unless, of course, he strings you along with a lie)!

So, you go out on a date, have a fabulous time, feel real chemistry for the guy, but it's been a week and you haven't heard from him yet. If a guy hasn't called after a week, *he's just not interested!* Women are always trying to analyze why a guy is not calling. Sometimes the woman wonders if she should call him. The answer is *no*. When a man is interested, he will not only call you, but he will make sure that you know he is interested. Oftentimes a man knows that he isn't interested in seeing a woman again, but he can't face rejecting or hurting her, so he just won't call. Most men aren't comfortable calling to say, "I had a great time, thanks and good luck, have a good life." Or, "You're really nice, but I just don't want to take you out again," especially when they run the risk of the woman confronting him and asking, "Why?"

Do not sit there and think of 101 reasons he may not be

calling. It's so tempting to make up excuses for the guy like, "He's so busy at work," or "He just got out of a long-term relationship and needs his space." Or my personal favorite, "He told me that he's in the middle of moving." But none of these excuses will stop a determined man. When a man meets the right woman, nothing stops him from calling or trying to see her. And nowadays with numerous means of contact—cell phones, faxes, BlackBerries, e-mail—there is no excuse for not getting in touch.

WHEN A GUY IS INTERESTED, HE WILL "RESERVE" YOU FOR HIMSELF

Ladies, ever try to figure out what's going on in a guy's head about how serious he is about you? Here's what guys say about how and when they know she's "The One."

1. "I just want to be with her. She is always on my mind, even when I am at work."
2. "I just get a gut feeling, like this girl is 'The One.'"
3. "I like the way my friends like her. They are always commenting, 'She's really a great girl,' or 'You two are really good together,' or 'She's really down to earth. Really nice and friendly.'"
4. "I feel like I can bring her home to meet my family and be proud."
5. "I just want to be with her, and only her."
6. "I like everything about her. I love the way she walks and carries herself. I love the way she smells. She's so feminine."
7. "I feel comfortable around her. I feel I can be myself."

8. "I feel like I want to protect her and do special things for her."

9. "She is so sexy, a real turn-on, and at the same time she is really classy and elegant. I am proud to show her off."

10. "I just love her looks, the way she smells, and how nicely she takes care of herself. It makes me think she'll always do that."

11. "I can really imagine her being the mother of my children."

WE HAD SUCH A GREAT TIME, BUT NOW SHE'S NOT CALLING ME BACK

Having a hard time figuring out the opposite sex isn't exclusive to women. Men, too, need to know "the signs" as to whether a woman is really interested. We all know about a guy not calling when he says he will and how frustrated the ladies get, but it happens to men all the time as well. And they are often pretty confused about it. I just got a call the other day from my client, Jim, who had a fabulous date with Veronica. When he asked her at the end of the evening if she would like to see him again, she said, "Yes, call me."

Jim later related to me, "Marla, I am so confused. I have called her for the past three days, but she has not returned my calls. Can you get me some feedback and see if she really wants to see me again or not?"

Gentlemen, I am going to give it to you straight! Women have a really hard time hurting someone's feelings or being put in an uncomfortable position. I am always happy to contact the woman and get feedback for my client, but it is usually pointless. The response is the same: "Jim was really sweet, but I am just not attracted to him physically." So she just doesn't return his calls. Or if she does happen to get caught on the phone or asked out again, she might say:

1. I have decided to get back together with my ex.

2. I am so busy at work right now that I really don't have time for a relationship.

3. I am going out of town for a couple of months. Maybe we can see each other when I get back.

4. I just met someone else and want to see how it goes with him.

5. I've decided that I am really not interested in being in a relationship at this point in my life.

These are all cop-outs. So guys, if a woman is not returning your calls, she is just not interested. She's never going to be your soul mate. It's time to move on.

SOUL MATE ASSIGNMENT

What "Lines" Have You Heard
from Someone Who Wasn't
Interested in Furthering a Relationship
(or What Lines Have You Used)?

CHAPTER 14
Enjoy the Ride!

Here is a recap of the most important "do's" to keep in mind. Refer to this list often to refresh your memory and spur you into action! First, the main steps:

For deliberate creation of what you want to attract into your life:

1. Identify what you *don't* want.

2. Then identify what you *do* want.

3. Find the "feeling place" of your want.

4. Expect, listen, and allow the universe to deliver.

Additional tips:

♥ Take time each day to dream, create, desire, and flow energy to those desires.

♥ Repeat affirmations several times per day about what you want and why. Get really excited about them and make sure good energy is flowing while saying them.

♥ Stay in the present. Your past does not equal your present or your future.

♥ Remember that you are the creator of your experience.

♥ Keep writing and revising incredible scripts. Make them outrageous, fun, and fantastic! Make sure you word them in the present tense—you already have what you desire.

♥ Be gentle with yourself, love yourself, and respect yourself.

♥ Know that what you desire is on its way to you.

♥ Think only about what you do want, not what you don't want.

♥ Remember, timing is everything, so be patient.

♥ See the beauty in all things. Notice flowers, architecture or a child's smile.

♥ Always reach for the feeling of joy and well-being, so you are always moving toward that which you desire.

♥ When emotions feel good, you are allowing the fulfillment of your desire. So *feel* good all the time!

♥ Talk about how good things are, not the opposite.

♥ Be open to meeting people who don't fit your usual "profile."

♥ Make sure that you look and feel your best. Evaluate what you "bring to the table."

♥ Work on being fun and easy-going. Be the type of person you would like to hang out with.

♥ Take time each day to be silent. Eliminate the drama from your everyday life.

♥ Appreciate the unique qualities in others.

♥ Enjoy your life. Cultivate other interests besides "soul mate hunting."

♥ Always be courteous and on time. Treat others the way you would like to be treated.

♥ Take time to give to yourself. Fill yourself up to fullness, so that you can overflow in giving to someone else.

♥ Remember that the way you think is the way you feel; the way you feel is the way you vibrate; the way you vibrate is the way you attract.

It's Your Canvas, Your Creation

You cannot go wrong. You cannot make a mistake. This idea of creating what you desire in your life through feelings might be new to you, but that's okay. It works! Have fun with it. Make a game out of it. Practice flowing energy, getting a buzz on, writing new scripts. Write your own affirmations and live in gratitude. Most of all, live in the present. Whatever happened or didn't happen in the past has nothing to do with now, unless you drag it there, which keeps your energy low.

Learn to *feel* your desires instead of just thinking about them. The world is your oyster. By learning to control the flow of your energy, you learn to take control of your life. You will get what you expect, so expect the best!

CHAPTER 15

Ask Marla
dating q&a's

One of my roles as a matchmaker is answering lots of questions and offering practical advice to help ensure the success of my clients. The following are some frequently asked questions about the dating and relationship process.

How Do I Make a Good Impression over the Phone?

For those of you going through a matchmaking service, your first contact with your match will be over the phone. This conversation is very important. It can determine whether or not you end up meeting at all. Unfortunately, many people are eliminated within the first few minutes of a phone call. I know that it can be daunting and a bit nerve-wracking to make contact with a stranger, and at the same time try to be charming and make a good impression. Your soul mate could be on the other end of the line! Here are a few tips to help make your first conversation go smoothly.

First, realize that the other person on the line might be a bit nervous and the person's true personality may not come through. Try to keep the conversation short so that when you do meet, you will have lots to talk about. Try to sound happy to hear from your match and excited about meeting. I have heard countless complaints from clients that their match seemed preoccupied, uninterested, or too busy to give them the time of day. If you are really serious about meeting someone special to spend your life with, treat everyone with respect and in the way that you want to be treated.

I had a man tell me that when he called his match, she seemed monotone and uninterested, asked him to call back later, and quickly got off the phone. When I spoke with her and asked if she was indeed interested in speaking with and meeting this gentleman, she replied, "Oh, absolutely! It's just that when he called, I was in the middle of a business meeting, so I couldn't talk." There are ways of letting a guy know that this is not a good time to talk without squashing his hopes! You can always say, "Hello, Jim. Wonderful to hear from you! I am right in the middle of a meeting, but look forward to speaking with you. What time would be good to call you back?"

One of the funniest ones I've heard was from a woman who returned a guy's call. They had a ten-minute conversation, but she felt that he was not too interested because his voice was so low and he seemed preoccupied. When I spoke to him, he told me that he was speaking that way because he was in a library. Well, he failed to communicate that with her!

Phone tag seems to be a problem these days. Everyone is so busy that it is easy to keep missing each other. I have heard about people playing phone tag for weeks without ever connecting. How frustrating! A lot of people figure that it's a lost cause, give up, and ask for another match. Not always a good idea. That could have been the perfect person for you. My remedy for phone tag is simple: leave a message for your match with a few possible times that you will be available to talk, have the person choose one, and leave you a message with the time. Voilà! You have a date!

How Do I Make a Good Impression on the First Date?

Come to the date with expectant energy. If you are going to make the effort and take the time to look nice, doesn't it make sense to also take the time to put yourself in the right frame of mind? This step is even more important than what outfit you're wearing or how nice your hair turned out. You can be Cindy Crawford, Tyra Banks, and Angelina Jolie all rolled into one, and it still won't guarantee that you will get asked out on a second date. Take some time before your date—it could be fifteen minutes, five minutes, or even three minutes—to sit down, close your eyes, take a deep breath, let Spirit in, and visualize just how you would like your evening to go.

Picture everything going smoothly. Picture yourself

having a pleasant time with this new person who might be nervous, excited, frustrated with dating, or all of the above and more. Let any past negative dating experiences go. They have no place in your heart or mind anymore. This is a new day, a new person, and a new chance. Affirm to yourself that your experience will be just great, and fill yourself with positive expectation. Affirm how wonderful and special you are and how deserving of a perfect relationship you are. You can also affirm and accept that if this person is not your soul mate, the right one is on the way. Recognize that each new person you meet can bring something interesting and wonderful to your life. For instance, on a date with Marcia during which you have no romantic chemistry, she is so impressed with your positive, upbeat, and fun personality that she wants to introduce you to her best friend Tina, who is also single and looking for Mr. Right! So, when you put yourself in a positive frame of mind before you even leave the house, you're ahead of the game.

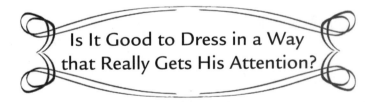

Is It Good to Dress in a Way that Really Gets His Attention?

Ladies, you definitely want to make a great first impression. As you know, men are visual creatures, and I have been told that they usually know within the first three seconds whether they are interested or not. Three seconds! Can you believe it? So that means your "look" can make or break it for you. I have met with women in the office who were very natural-looking, wearing light makeup and very pretty. Then when I got feedback from the gentlemen they had met, they reported back that although she was very nice, she was so overly made-up that it was a real turn-off. In trying to look pretty for a date, it's possible to go overboard. Most men prefer a fresh-faced beauty. Some makeup is nice, but don't overdo it. The same applies to perfume. Less is more. Everyone has different tastes, so until you know his, go lightly with the perfume. Something feminine and clean smelling is your best bet. Some ladies tend to spray on half a bottle of something very strong and overpowering just before walking out the door. You don't want to give your date a headache or a sneezing attack.

Now, let's talk about clothing. What you wear on a first date can also be crucial. Aim for something comfortable, classy, understated, elegant, and feminine. These are all great words to describe the look you should be going for. It's not wise to wear an ultra-mini skirt and a skimpy top with your cleavage spilling out. You will look trashy. He might think that you'll be fun for the night, but would not want to take you home to meet his mother. If you have a nice figure, definitely wear something that shows it. I have heard countless times from men that on the first date, and often the second as well, they had no idea what her figure was like because she wore something so shapeless and baggy. Be sure that you wear something as feminine as possible. Also, ask your date about the event that you are going to. Will you need park clothes, beachwear, or rock-climbing gear? If you are going to the zoo and will be walking all day, you won't want to show up in high heels.

You'd be surprised at how proper attire can make or break a date. Harold invited Liz to go to an art show and then a long walk through the park. She showed up in a blouse and skirt and designer high heels. He was frustrated because she couldn't walk long in them. He offered to take her home to pick up a pair of tennis shoes, but she told him that she didn't own any. He offered to take her to a sporting goods store to buy her some, but she felt funny about it and declined. So not only could they not go to the show as planned, but the whole mood of the date was broken. Harold later told me that he prefers a woman who is more down-to-earth, someone who can put on a pair of slacks and some tennis shoes and go with the flow.

Who Pays for What and Why?

If you are part of an upscale matchmaking service, especially the kind where the ladies don't have to pay to join, you know it is customary for the man to pay for the date. But if you are Internet dating, you should probably expect to pay half. Many times it is just easier to go for coffee. Men's and women's roles are a bit mixed up these days. Women want equality in every area, but when it comes to dating, we still love to be treated like a lady, be protected and be taken care of. A lot of women will "test" a guy when the check comes. She'll pull out her wallet and say, "How much do I owe?" If he lets her pay half, she finds him cheap and probably would not see him again.

When I was dating, I never knew what to do. After my divorce, I remember asking a single woman who dated a lot, "Will he pay for dinner?" She told me that the man is lucky to be having dinner with such a beautiful, fascinating woman, and he should be glad to pay for dinner! So, I went with that advice and it worked pretty well. But you don't want to just take all the time. If you continue to see a man, it would be nice to treat him once in a while, or invite him to your place and cook for him. I did that with my now-husband. For the first couple of weeks, he wined and dined me. Then I wanted to reciprocate and would cook for him a couple of nights per week. I'm a vegetarian and one of my specialties was a vegetable stir-fry with tofu. I thought it was quite tasty and thought that he did, too. He actually hated it, but was too polite to say anything until a couple of years later! He silently suffered through my tofu stir-fry just to spend time with me.

So, ladies, go ahead and let the man pay for dinner or drinks, but show your appreciation with a sincere thank-you, and if you continue to see each other, give him a treat once in a while.

Is It Okay to Have Sex on the First Date if It Feels Right?

You have probably heard the saying, "Never sleep with someone on the first date!" If you think that you might have some interest in a person for the long term, do not sleep with him or her on the first, second, or even third date. Most men subscribe to the idea that if a woman sleeps with him right away, she probably makes a habit of it. Recently, Carla called me up after meeting a gorgeous man that I had introduced her to. "Bingo!" she shouted into the phone. "He is wonderful! We had such an incredible time! We had lots of chemistry, but I remembered what you told me about not sleeping with a guy too soon, and it was so hard for me. I had so much chemistry and it was so hard to resist, but I didn't do it." I applauded her and advised her not to sleep with him until they were in an exclusive relationship.

When two people get intimate immediately, they miss out on all the courting, flirting, falling for each other, and that wonderful time of discovering each other. They suddenly find themselves catapulted ahead to "boyfriend and girlfriend," but they don't even know each other. Then it is a very awkward situation, and neither knows how to behave. And, ladies, you definitely run the risk of the guy never calling you again.

Women Want Equality, So Why Do They Still Expect Men to Open the Door and Do All Sorts of Things for Them?

When a man opens the car door for a woman, it's not because she is too weak to do it herself. He does it to show that he cares. He does it to let her know that she is special. When the woman feels this again and again on a date, she begins to relax because it feels good and nurturing. The modern woman has many needs. Here are a few:

1. She needs someone who cares about her well-being and seeks to understand her feelings.

2. She needs someone to help her and support her through life so that she doesn't feel like she is going it alone.

3. She needs attention from someone whom she feels truly cares about her.

4. She needs to know that her feelings of love are returned.

5. She needs someone to take the lead in making plans.

Is Honesty Really the Best Policy?

Lately, I have been getting a lot of calls from guys regarding "flaky" women. I heard three frustrating stories in one week that I am going to tell you about. The first one is about a very sweet gentleman named Joe who had a date set with Cindy. Cindy even confirmed by calling Joe to ask if they could meet one hour later that night because she had something to do. He complied and went to pick her up at 7:45. He arrived at her door and knocked, but there was no answer. He knocked some more and even called her name. The lights in the house were on and the dogs were barking. Joe got on his cell and called her. There was no answer. She totally stood him up. He was so frustrated!

The next guy, Peter, had a second date set for a Saturday night with Pamela. He arrived at her house with a bouquet of roses. He knocked on the door. No answer. He called her on his cell. She answered. She told him that she had her period and could not go out. He heard noise in the background like she was in a restaurant. He was furious!

Then there is Scott. He had a Monday night date set with Julia. They spoke on Friday, and decided on the time and place. She actually insisted on a certain restaurant that she was familiar with and he agreed. Scott called Julia on Sunday just to confirm. He got her machine, so he left a message that he would see her the next night. She did not call him back, so the next night he got a babysitter for his son and drove twenty miles to meet her. She never showed up or even called. Needless to say, he was angry, frustrated, and hurt.

I have been giving a lot of thought as to why people are so afraid of being honest. Why are we not just able to say, "Look, you're probably a super nice guy, but I just don't care for your voice on the phone, and I don't think that I want to meet you after all." Or, "I had a really great time with you, but I don't feel any physical chemistry. Thanks for everything. I wish you the best." But instead, we stand people up, avoid their calls, or make up silly excuses.

We are so worried about hurting someone's feelings or looking like "the bad guy" that we do not allow ourselves to be authentic and honest. I have been on both ends myself. I used to make up stupid stories to get out of going on a date with a guy. I also remember really liking a certain guy that I had been out with a couple of times. We had a date set for one evening. I was really excited. I got all dressed up and was sitting there waiting. He was supposed to pick me up at 7:30. Well, 7:30 came and went, and so did 8:30, 9:30, and 10:30. I went to bed in tears. We should be able to communicate with each other. There are ways in which to be honest, and yet tasteful and caring at the same time.

I recently introduced Will and Lena. After their first date, Will e-mailed me to say how excited he was to get to know her better. He said there was definitely chemistry. Lena also expressed how much she liked Will and was excited to see him again. Lena was forty-four, and Will was sixty-five. Age was not a problem for Lena, as she liked older men. A few weeks went by, and they saw each other a few more times. Then I got an e-mail from Will asking me if I had any feedback for him regarding Lena. He felt that she had cooled a bit. I gave her a call, and she told me that although he was fabulous and had all of the qualities she was looking in a man, he was almost a dead ringer for her father. She said that it was not the age; it was his looks and even the way he carried himself. She just could not "go there." She told me that she was planning to call him and make up some excuse—like she met someone else or that she was just too busy to date now. I asked her, "Why not just tell the truth? He can't help it if he looks like your father. He would appreciate knowing the real reason. I am certain of it." Of course, Will would have been disappointed either way, whether Lena told him the truth or made something up, so why not just be honest? People really appreciate being told the truth, even if it hurts a little bit. It helps them with dating in the future, and they respect a person who is honest. The old adage, "Honesty is the best policy," really is true.

When Is the Best Time to Become Exclusive?

When giving advice to my women members about dating, I always tell them to "date like a guy" until they have a commitment. So often I'll get a phone call or an e-mail that goes something like this: "Hi, Marla. Hey, thanks for all of your help. I've been on some really great dates, but I just met a guy last week at a party. We've only been out once, but I really like him, so I think I'll hold off on dating anyone else and see how it goes with him." Or, "Hi, Marla. Wow, thanks for introducing me to Mark. He's everything I'm looking for, so you can put me on hold."

No! No! No! Why put all of your eggs in one basket after one date, or even a few dates for that matter? Ladies, you can be sure that the guys are not operating that way. Sure, it does happen occasionally that two people just click from the get-go and are inseparable from then on . . . actually, that's what happened with me and my husband . . . but more often than not, the guy is still looking around to see if there's anything better out there, and he's testing the waters with you while keeping his options open. It just kills me when a woman puts herself on hold when she's seeing a guy, but I know that he is not exclusive with her because he is still calling me to match him up! Until you have a commitment from a guy, my advice is to continue to date like a guy. That way you won't waste your time or get as hurt if he decides to move on.

Also, talk of becoming exclusive or marriage, or declaring your love too soon, almost always ends in disaster. I matched up Emily and Greg recently. Greg lives in Miami, and Emily lives in L.A. Greg is going to be bi-coastal soon because of his business and is fine with meeting women from L.A. Greg came to town and took Emily out to a nice dinner and then to a jazz club afterward. They really hit it off. He liked her a lot and even mentioned her coming to Miami to visit him. He left to go back home the next day, but called her twice a day for a week. They really were enjoying getting to know each other. Greg bought Emily a ticket to come and visit him just ten days after they met. She was ecstatic and hopped on the plane! Emily was there with him about five days when Greg called me. He told me that she is a lovely, warm, wonderful woman and that they were having a fabulous time together. She was crazy about his dog, loved his house, was easy-going, and fit right in with everything. But he was completely turned off when she told him that she loved him and started talking marriage. They had only known each other a little over two weeks! He felt too much pressure and decided to break things off. If Emily had let things progress naturally and just enjoyed her time with Greg, who knows how it would have turned out? But the way she handled things guaranteed Greg running for the hills. So ladies, keep your cool, take your time, enjoy the process, and date like a guy!

If My Date Is Creepy, Is It Okay to Just Exit Out the Back Door without Saying Good-Bye?

I recently received a call from a male client giving me feedback on his date the night before. Ronald had invited Stella to a lovely restaurant downtown with a beautiful outdoor patio and a fountain. They were seated, and ordered a glass of wine and some appetizers. Ronald found Stella to be attractive, but a bit standoffish. He thought the conversation was going pretty well, and they ordered another glass of wine. Then Stella excused herself to go to the ladies' room.

After about fifteen minutes, Ronald started to become

concerned. He got up and started looking around the restaurant. He asked the host and waiter if they had seen her, but neither had. He went back to the table and waited another fifteen minutes, and then he called her on his cell. He left her a couple of messages with no response. He finally went home. He had met her at the restaurant so he did not know her address. He was very worried about her and considered calling the police. I told him that I would call her and try to find out what happened. I called her three times with no response and e-mailed her twice.

After a few days, I was also very concerned, so I left another message on her voice mail informing her that if I did not hear from her by the next day, I would be calling the police and have them go to her home. Well, she immediately e-mailed me, apologizing for not responding. She said she had found Ronald unattractive. He had some strange dental work in his teeth, and she couldn't look at him. She said that she did not know what to do, so she pretended to go to the ladies' room and just left. I was astounded. I felt so badly for Ronald, as he was truly concerned about Stella and couldn't believe that she would walk out without a word. He was so embarrassed and hurt.

The best thing to do in a situation where you just do not want to be there is to simply cut the evening short by saying that you are terribly sorry but you do not feel that you two are a good match. Then thank him for his time and understanding and wish him the best. There is no reason to hurt someone's feelings by walking out on your date.

Help! Dating Has Become a Full-Time Job!

If you are involved with a dating service or an Internet site, you just might have more dates than you can handle! Jay was on two different Internet sites and very serious about finding a partner, so he was going on about ten coffee dates per week. As you can imagine, he got burned out pretty quickly. He was not only getting tired of repeating the story of his life to each woman, but he was having trouble remembering with whom he had been out with and their story. He also became very discouraged and down on himself that he was not finding the right chemistry with someone. Jay definitely needed to take a "time out" from dating.

Sometimes we tend to put a lot of pressure on ourselves when it comes to finding the right person, and we feel that we should be out dating as much as possible in order to accomplish that mission. It can be very advantageous to take some time for you and not go on any dates for a certain amount of time to regroup and maintain a positive attitude.

Julia had some interesting feedback on Charles. She said that although she found him to be very attractive and a nice person, she just felt that he was going through the motions and seemed a bit bitter and jaded. They had dinner plans, but when they got to the restaurant, Charles suggested that they just have a drink at the bar. Julia got the idea that he did this in order to check her out to see if he thought she was good enough for him to actually spend the money for dinner on her. Charles also told Julia that he had been on numerous dates through the matchmaking service. Nothing was working out, and he was getting fed up with it. Charles not only ruined his chances with Julia, but he also wasted their time. Charles really needed to take a "time out" from dating for a while to get his confidence and positive attitude back. It's also a good idea to take a "time out" after a breakup, especially if it was a long relationship or a very emotional or difficult breakup. This will give you some time to heal, and you won't be as likely to talk about your ex all night to your date.

If the Date Was So Great, Why Doesn't He Call Again?

I know from my conversations with my male clients that even a seemingly small thing can be the deciding factor for a guy as to whether he will call again. He might decide against calling after thinking about it for a few days. For example, maybe the woman was looking around the room too much at dinner and didn't seem focused on him. Maybe she wore too much makeup, was twenty minutes late without calling, made negative remarks about children and he has two kids . . . it could be anything. And unless you are fortunate enough to have a matchmaker who can get honest feedback for you, you probably will never know the reason. The other day I had a guy decide not to call a woman because she has a small dog. He feels that women with small dogs love their dogs more than the man in their life. Another guy had one date with a woman, went to her apartment afterward, and saw that she didn't have any furniture. "Not one stick," he said. He told me that he could not date a woman who did not have any furniture because it showed that she didn't have her act together. And yet another guy told me recently that although the woman he met was sweet and attractive, she had bad oral hygiene—some gum recession and yellowing of her teeth—and he could not picture kissing her.

When I was dating, I also had a hard time understanding why on earth a man would say he would call and then never did! I remember having dates that were so much fun! I knew that he was having a great time as well. There would even be chemistry—maybe we were kissing and flirting a lot—and then the end of the evening would come and he'd say, "I had a great time. I'll call you." I'd coo, "Me too," and be on cloud nine, so excited that I'd had such a wonderful time with a great guy who wanted to see me again. The next day would come, and no call from him. *Well,* I thought to myself, *he's probably busy with work. He'll call tomorrow.* Tomorrow came, and still no call. A week went by, and another and another. Well, I would finally realize, this "great" guy would not be calling.

I remember an especially hurtful situation in which I dated a guy a few times and then (stupidly) spent the night with him. The next day he hugged and kissed me passionately and said, "I'll call you tomorrow." I felt very secure and confident. He did not call the next day or the next. I finally called him at work. He told me he was in a meeting and would call me back. He never did. I tried once more a few days later. He gave me the same story, and then didn't call me again. I felt like a complete fool! I thought that I must have done something wrong or that something must be wrong with me. I now know that the reason men say "I'll call you" upon their exit from a date when they really have no intention of doing so is simply because, for whatever reason, they do not feel the chemistry for a long-term relationship with you, but they do not want to hurt your feelings or have an awkward or unpleasant moment.

It does not matter how good a time you had or how much chemistry you thought was there. They have a reason, and you might never find out what it is, but they are just not interested in pursuing you any further. They don't mean to be jerks; it's just that they don't know what else to do. Women do the same thing. They may tell a guy, "Sure, I'd love to see you again. Call me." But when he does call her, she never returns his call, hoping that he'll get "the hint." I have been guilty of that myself in the past, not wanting to hurt the guy's feelings. If your date doesn't call again, that person is not for you, simple as that. Chalk it up to a good time and move on!

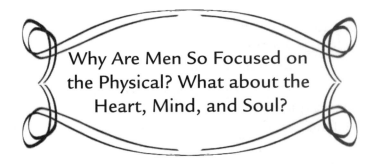

Why Are Men So Focused on the Physical? What about the Heart, Mind, and Soul?

Day in and day out, I hear men tell me they are looking for a "10"! Even if they themselves are a "4," they still expect that a much younger, drop-dead-gorgeous woman is the least they deserve. God bless them, but that is the most frustrating part of my job! And many women ask me, "Are looks all that these men are interested in? Do they just want a trophy wife? What about the soul . . . don't they care about that?"

Yes, men can seem very shallow, judging a woman solely on her looks. In the specialized service that I work for, I do feel terrible turning away fabulous women because I know that my male clients would not want to meet them based on their appearance. And because the men in my service are paying a lot, they expect the moon. Men's preferences are biologically hardwired to find signs of youth and health attractive in order to determine which females are best suited to carry on their genes. It might sound silly and unfair, but men just can't help it. Men are visual. Women, on the other hand, are more attracted to other qualities in a man, such as the way he makes a woman feel. Have you ever noticed that you see a lot more average and unattractive men with beautiful women than the other way around? Exactly! We will never change our "shallow" brothers. We must embrace them and sometimes have a good laugh about the absurdity of it all!

But, at the same time, don't throw in the towel just because you don't look like Pam Anderson. Neither do I, but my husband thinks I'm a "10." And most men really are looking for the "whole package." The most important thing is that you feel good about yourself. If that means getting into better shape or updating your appearance, it can only help you to be more attractive to a man.

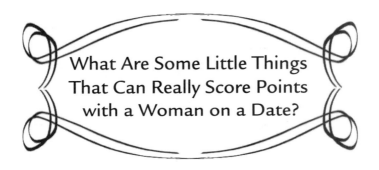

What Are Some Little Things That Can Really Score Points with a Woman on a Date?

There are a few things that really make a guy stand out above the rest of the competition, and they are very simple. Chivalry may seem to be a thing of the past, but women love an old-fashioned gentleman. It might sound silly to mention this, but many men, especially younger ones, don't think about this. Guys, walk a lady to her car. It shows that you are a gentleman and care about her safety. On the same subject, I heard a story from a woman who had a lovely dinner with a guy; she really liked him and was sorry that the evening was ending. They walked outside to the valet, and her date asked her, "Do you have your ticket?" Thinking that he was going to take it from her and take care of it, she held it up for him. But instead, he just said, "Good," and then proceeded to get into his car and drive off! He realized what he had done the next day and apologized over the phone, but it had made a negative impression on her. Paying a woman's valet ticket is very considerate and a nice touch.

If you have hit it off on the phone and are really looking forward to the date, showing up with flowers or a little gift is a winner. Compliment her on her outfit or hair. You can't go wrong.

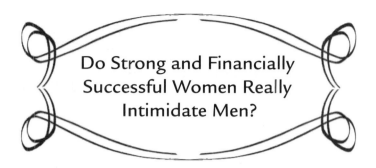

Do Strong and Financially Successful Women Really Intimidate Men?

For years, financially successful women have told me that they have trouble getting into a relationship because most men are intimidated by their success. It isn't the fact that the woman makes a high salary. The men that I meet appreciate that. They like the fact that a woman is not trying to get her hand in his wallet, but can take care of herself. They like dating intelligent, capable women. The problem arises for strong, assertive, independent, and successful women when the very characteristics that make them successful at work can make them unsuccessful in relationships. A man wants to feel that he is doing the pursuing. Don't behave in the dating arena the same way you behave in the business world. Let the man take the lead. Men like to feel needed and capable. You can make all of the money you want, climb the corporate ladder, and be tough as nails on the job, but when you are with him, let yourself be soft and feminine.

If He's So Great, Then Why Is He Single?

Many times when I call up a woman to tell her about a guy that I have in mind for her, she will say, "Well, if he's so great, then why is he single?" Oh boy, I have to tell you that this question really gets me going! Just because a man might be gorgeous, wealthy, and dynamic, and have a great sense of humor does not guarantee that he had time for or has found the right woman yet. He still has to go through the dating process, weeding through and trying on different hats to find the right fit. Many wonderful men out there are just busy. If they are successful financially, they are working their buns off. By the end of the day, they might go to the gym, go home, heat up a frozen dinner, watch the news, hit the hay, get up, and do it all over again. Actually, that sounds a lot like my life (except the frozen dinner). We are all working incredibly hard.

When I met my husband, he was forty-one and had never been married. For me it was a real treat, since I had been married twice already and had enough baggage to open a luggage shop. He was forty-three when he married me, and I feel very special because there were several women who had tried to pin him down over the years. But he was waiting for me, and that all comes back to timing.

Should I Change My Personality to Be More Attractive to Others?

I remember being at a girlfriend's house one day. Her name was Mary. She lived in a duplex on the ground floor. Her upstairs neighbor was a dishy single doctor, Dan, whom she had a crush on. But the doctor was dating Greta. Mary took note of how Greta dressed and behaved. She didn't know her, but would see her coming in and out of his place. Mary made assumptions about what kind of a girl Greta was and how that must be what Dan was interested in. Mary would even put her ear to the wall and listen to their conversations that filtered down.

She told me, "Greta sounds like a ding-a-ling! Maybe that's what men want. Should I change my personality? Maybe that's why I'm single. I need to act more ding-y or coquettish. Should I change my personality?"

Well, I really thought she'd lost it. I told her, "How on earth are you going to change your personality for each guy and keep it up? You might as well be Sybil!" Now I do believe there are certain things that everyone can change personality-wise to have a better chance at getting into a relationship. For example, we can learn not to talk too much about past relationships or not push for a relationship too soon. But your own personality is something special and unique. No one else is quite like you. The right man will fall in love with everything about you. Remember that Billy Joel song? "Don't go changin' to try to please me . . . I love you just the way you are!"

Sometimes I catch my husband watching me, and he'll

say, "You are quite an interesting character!" And I just say, "Thank you!" I know that I am unique and wouldn't want to be like anyone else. Rejoice in being quirky. Celebrate your intelligence, appreciate your humor, and show your style!

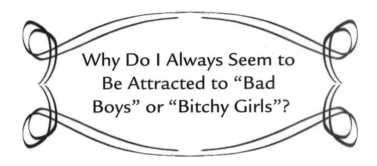

Why Do I Always Seem to Be Attracted to "Bad Boys" or "Bitchy Girls"?

You know the saying, "Nice guys finish last." I remember when I was dating in my twenties, and every time I told a guy he was "nice," he would wince and say, "Oh, no! Don't tell me that. Nice is no good!" And he was right. If I told a guy that he was "nice" it meant that I was not interested in him romantically. I remember quite a few "nice" guys who were crazy about me, even wanted to marry me—good solid guys who would have treated me like a queen and loved me forever. But at that time I wasn't into "nice" guys. I liked the "bad boys." The crappier they treated me, the more interested I became. If a guy stood me up, didn't call when he said he would call, cheated on me, told me I was fat, ooh, I just had to have him! It just made him seem so unattainable and sexy that I was up for the challenge! Men often do the same thing when it comes to women who treat them poorly. It becomes a contest to "conquer" this seemingly unattainable beauty.

"Bad boys" and "bitchy girls" are almost always the really

good-looking ones who have a million other girls and guys after them so they quickly realize they don't have to stick with one person. They can play the field because there will always be another sucker coming along any minute. The "bad boy" is like a kid in a candy store. One week he loves lemon drops, and then he tastes some gummy bears and decides he likes them better. Until he gets hold of some Sweet Tarts, and he's dropping the lemon drops and the gummy bears. Fortunately for them, most women in their twenties like "bad boys." They want to be with a "hot" guy, and dealing with the "bad boy" aspect is just something that comes with the territory. But when women get into their thirties—and have been burned a few too many times—they slowly start changing their tune.

I hear so often from women when I ask them what type of guy they are looking to meet, "Well, when I was in my twenties, looks were so important, but now I really just want a nice, good guy to settle down with. Looks are not first on my list anymore. I want to be treated well and appreciated." And then, of course, the ladies in their forties and up really get it and are looking for more of a certain level of lifestyle rather than a Brad Pitt look-alike. In a sense, they have learned to value the more soulful qualities of others, instead of superficialities like appearance.

I do find it very interesting that most of us, both men and women, go through the phase of allowing ourselves to be treated less well than we deserve. Low self-esteem often plays a big role. But I did find that because I was involved with so many "bad boys" over the years that when my husband came along, I was finally ready for a genuinely good guy, and I could appreciate him because I had something to compare him with.

Am I Giving Too Much Too Soon?

Giving too much too soon is a huge relationship mistake made by both men and women. At first, doing too much seems natural and fun. Aren't you supposed to do lots of special things for your new love? Aren't you supposed to go over the top to show just how much you care and how special and thoughtful you are? *No!* At least, not until your relationship reaches a certain point. Before that point, you risk suffocating your partner just as love is starting to blossom. It must happen naturally.

Too much commitment too soon shows desperation. If a person is ready to forsake all others without even being asked, hoping that this will somehow form a bond with the other person, it does just the opposite. Unless you have discussed it and have both decided to be in an exclusive relationship, never tell him that he is the only one in your life. You want to seem busy and in demand. I know this might seem like game-playing, but it is human nature to want something that is not available or a challenge to get.

Also, don't give her too much information about yourself right away. Tell her about yourself a little bit at a time. Don't be an open book. If the partner hears about things that you have done or accomplishments you have made through the grapevine, it will certainly pique her interest and she'll want to know more. Keep a bit of mystery about yourself.

Giving gifts can really make a man uncomfortable. A man once told me, "The minute a woman starts giving me gifts, I feel pressured. She appears like a needy woman who is trying to buy love." Put off gift-giving as long as possible. Show him that you care in other ways. For example, make him a lovely dinner, give him a ride when his car is in the shop, or offer to pick up his mail when he is out of town. And if his birthday comes around early on in the relationship, make it something with little monetary value. Don't try to impress him with how much you have spent. Instead, impress him with your creativity. I know a woman who doesn't make much money, but she wanted to get her guy something special. She went online and found a type of amusement park that has go-carts to race and lots of fun stuff that her guy was into. An all-day pass was only twenty bucks, so she printed out the ad from the place and made a cute card with the ad in it, letting him know that she was going to take him there for the day.

You can give your all when you have both made a mutual commitment. But even then, you will be wise to keep a bit of mystery to yourself as well. You will remain interesting and alluring to your mate.

Is a Man Not in Love If I Don't Get Romantic Gifts?

I had heard this theory before, and I had a chance to test it out myself with Mike from Chicago. We had been seeing each other for a few months, and my birthday was approaching. I thought that I had mentioned when it was at some point, but I was not sure if he remembered so I did something really goofy and tricky! I put out some birthday cards that people had sent me the year before, and I displayed about four or five of them on the table next to the sofa so he would think that I was getting birthday cards and would realize that it was coming up. Well, my birthday came, and not only did I not get a gift, but I didn't even get a phone call! It was like he purposely ignored the fact. I was really shocked and hurt. About three days later, he dropped by with a big box all wrapped with a red bow. "I'm sorry it's late," he said sheepishly. "I didn't know what to get you." I sat down and tore off the wrapping. "Wow, a toaster!" I exclaimed with a frozen smile. "How wonderful! Thank you!" He said proudly, "It's a four-slice toaster. Look . . . crumb trays!"

Well, needless to say, it wasn't long before he stopped calling and the whole thing just fizzled out! He didn't care enough to call or see me on my birthday, let alone get me a romantic gift or card. All he could come up with was a toaster, and three days late no less! I guess that meant our relationship was toast!

When a man is in love with you and thinks about you in a romantic way, he will want to show you on special occasions. He will find a way to discover what you like and to show his feelings. When dating, kitchen appliances don't spell l-o-v-e.

How Can I Tell If He or She Is "The One"?

Ask yourself the following questions to find out if a certain person is ready for *you!*

♥ Do you spend a lot of time by the phone, waiting for a call?

♥ Do you go out mostly during the week, like Mondays or Thursdays, but never seem to snag a weekend date?

♥ Does the person call you mostly in the mid-morning, during commercials when watching TV, or late at night when it's too late to go out?

♥ When he does call, does he give you feeble excuses for not calling sooner, like, "I've been really busy lately"?

♥ Does she act "touchy," change the subject, or ignore you when you discuss nailing down future plans?

♥ Does he prefer to e-mail, rather than speak in person?

♥ Do her plans always involve something she wants to do and then she says, "Come along if you want to" (like she's granting you a privilege)?

♥ Does he tell you he'll have to "wait and see" when you ask him to join you for a special event?

♥ Does he frequently not call when he says he will?

♥ Do you have to take the initiative all the time to get together?

♥ Do you feel like you're trying too hard to keep her interested?

♥ Does he talk about his future plans, like moving or buying a house, that clearly don't include you?

♥ Do you always meet at your place, but rarely at hers?

♥ Is she reluctant to introduce you to her friends or family?

♥ Does he pick you up for a date, or does he expect you to meet him out?

♥ When he is talking to friends on the phone in your presence, does he conveniently leave out the fact that he is with you when they clearly ask him what he is doing?

♥ Does he call mostly late at night, asking to come over and "see you" . . . in other words, is the connection between you mostly based on "free sex"?

♥ Does he often "forget" his wallet when it's time to pay the bill at dinner?

If you answered "yes" to two or more of these questions, it's very possible this person is not interested in a long-term relationship, at least not with you. If you're looking for someone to settle down with, then it's time to move on! Some people think if they just stick around long enough, it will only be a matter of time before the person will "change" because of their growing love. But this is rarely the case. If his actions aren't showing his interest in you early on, when he is most likely to make the effort to try to impress you, then chances are they won't change later when he's even more likely to take your devotion for granted.

Ask yourself the questions above early in any relationship to help you assess if it's time to move on so as not to waste your time or risk getting your heart broken. To hedge your bets, until a partner has asked you to be "exclusive," feel free to date others. Go out, have fun, meet and experience new people! Don't put all of your eggs in one basket.

When a person feels that you are too eager, desperate, or just waiting around for her, she will run as fast as a turkey on Thanksgiving! When it's right, you won't have to force or push anything. It will feel as though it was really meant to be, because it is!

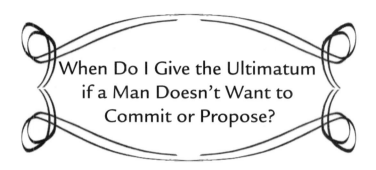

When Do I Give the Ultimatum if a Man Doesn't Want to Commit or Propose?

If marriage is your priority, then treat it as such. If the man you are dating seems uninterested in making a commitment or has made comments against marriage, don't just wait around hoping that he will eventually change his way of thinking. The man I was dating before I met my husband did exactly that. I felt that we got along great and had a lot of passion and fun together, but in front of me he would make anti-marriage comments. One in particular blew me away. He was on the telephone talking to his buddy who was getting married in a few weeks. Mark was going to be his best man. He was telling him, "Hey, John, it's not too late to get out of it, you know." I could tell that John was saying something like, "Oh, no, I don't want to get out of it!" But Mark kept pushing, saying, "Are you sure? Come on, you don't have to do this." It was really weird, but a clear sign of where our own relationship was going—nowhere! So, don't just stay in limbo. You have to discuss your goal of marriage. When you don't clarify your goals at a relatively early stage, it's easy to get caught up in the relationship, and it makes it harder to leave if he isn't looking for the same things that you are. If the two of you are not on the same wavelength in terms of marriage, it is best to stop it before you both get too emotionally invested in something that is going nowhere.

APPENDIX A

Affirmations

My "attracting magnet" is powerfully turned on with emotionally charged, positive vibrations, and I attract all that I desire into my life.

Love pours into my life from every corner of the universe. I know that I am loved.

I am clear in the process of attracting all that I want into my life.

- ♥ Identify what I *don't* want.
- ♥ Then identify what I *do* want.
- ♥ Get into the "feeling place" of what I want.
- ♥ Expect, listen, and allow it to happen.

I do not dwell on the past. Each new day brings the possibility of love and blessings.

All "don't wants" are banished from my awareness. I state my "do wants" clearly and with powerful feelings behind them.

My "do wants" are big in quality as well as quantity! I am constantly creating new wants and desires.

I am safe. I am constantly creating my own safety through my energy flow.

I keep my buzz on all day long! I keep my frequencies up and my valve open. Low frequencies are not welcome in my energy field.

I am excited about my "do wants." I am always writing new and exciting scripts that make me feel warm and fuzzy.

Mistakes don't bother me. If I mess up, I get right back on track. I am gentle with myself.

I live in the now with great expectations for the future.

I never give up on things that are important to me. I can't win if I don't play.

Other people's negative energy does not affect me. Their negative thoughts do not penetrate my energy field.

I know that my soul mate is on the way to me now.

I begin each new day with a positive outlook. I intend for wonderful things to happen.

I am always open to new ideas. I have an open mind and an open heart.

I see the good in others and give other people a chance. I choose not to judge.

I am vibrationally pulling in the perfect mate for me.

I have wonderful, creative ideas, and people are interested in what I have to say.

I don't tell anyone what I don't have. I tell myself what I do have.

I have all that I need right here and now. I am complete and whole.

I take extremely good care of my beautiful self.

I have my own interests and hobbies. A soul mate in my life is icing on the cake!

I am intelligent and capable. People respect my feelings and opinions.

I turn every challenge into an opportunity.

I deserve to be loved, and I know that I am loveable.

Letting go doesn't mean giving up. I release and I let go, knowing that my highest good is on its way.

I hold my vision of attracting my soul mate into my life. I do not waver in my faith.

I let go of my attachment of meeting the

right person in order to meet the right person.

I am always in the right place at the right time.

I am worthy of a healthy, respectful relationship.

I treat myself with kindness and expect the same of others.

I am beautiful and inspirational. I am a work of art.

I give myself permission to be in a loving relationship. I deserve the best!

Dating is fun and an adventure. I treat each new date as an opportunity to meet someone new and interesting.

When I tune in, turn on, and feel good, I open my magic valve and let my high-vibrational flow flood through me.

I am constantly writing new scripts and thinking of new and fresh ways to attract what I want into my life.

I enjoy the journey as much as the destination. I am having fun on the path to meeting my soul mate.

My life is drama-free. I am centered and at peace.

The right person shows up at the right time. Timing is everything.

Love is all around me. I choose to see the love.

Love radiates from every cell of my body. I send love out into the world, and it is mirrored back to me.

The right person for me appreciates my uniqueness and creativity.

I know that I am fully supported by the universe. I am worthy of all good things just because I am me.

I am special and unique; there is no one else like me.

Add your own affirmations:

_____

_____

_____

_____

_____

_____

_____

How a Matchmaking Service Can Help You Find Your Soul Mate

There are a lot of options for finding that special someone. Often, people who want a little help will turn to a dating service or a matchmaking service. So, what's the difference between the two?

A dating service lets members choose their own matches. A dating service generally takes on as many people as possible, and you have to go to the office and select someone you would like to meet and who is willing to meet you. Because it always involves photos, usually a small percentage of the "hottest" members get selected the most. That's great for them, but there are lots of other great people who get overlooked.

In a matchmaking service, professional matchmakers actually match you with other members. They do all of the work for you, which is great for busy professionals. At your initial meeting, they sit down with you and get to know your personality, interests, and hobbies and what you are looking for in a partner. Then they take it from there and select someone for you to meet whom they feel is compatible. Based on your criteria, they rule out people you would not be interested in meeting. Also, the matchmakers get valuable feedback from both members after the first date, helping them to get closer to a perfect match. Naturally, as a professional matchmaker, I'm a huge advocate of this type of service over a dating service.

Top Ten Reasons to Use a Matchmaking Service

1. Dates are screened in advance, so you're not wasting time with people with whom you have nothing in common. A service screens out what you don't want and tries to match what you do want (such as faith-based values, a certain age range, income, lifestyle, etc.).

2. Today's singles seem to have limited time for meeting other singles and dating. Who wants to spend an evening with someone who's not interesting to you? A service increases the likelihood that you won't be wasting time with inappropriate dates.

3. Services are great for people who are new to a particular area. If you have just moved somewhere, you probably don't know where to meet appropriate singles, and you haven't found any groups to join yet, such as professional organ-

izations and churches. A service can introduce you to the best people in your new hometown.

4. It's tough these days to find the best places to meet people. Maybe your church, volunteer organization, or Rotary group just hasn't come through for you in revealing suitable dates. It's time to hand the search over to a matchmaking service!

5. Many people feel uncomfortable meeting singles in bars or crowded events. Sure, "good" people also go to bars and clubs, but you have to weed through a *lot* of poor matches to try to find the "cream of the crop." Why waste your time? Let a matchmaking service weed through the masses for you.

6. It's expensive to date these days. There is the cost of restaurants, parking, alcohol, clothing, tips, and so on. It adds up when you are dating a series of people with no potential. Using a matchmaking service can be easier and cheaper than going on a thousand dates and not finding someone right for you.

7. Once you meet someone, there's always the "grilling" process where you ask each other lots of questions to find out if you are compatible. Matchmakers can significantly reduce this process for you. Don't like pets? A matchmaker will screen that out for you right away. You won't have to spend an evening with someone only to find out she has five cats at home.

8. We are all busy these days, especially with our careers. Often, we just want to go home, relax on the couch, and watch TV! Of course, we have to get out to meet people, but if we do it on our own we may find ourselves going home time after time wishing we had just stayed home!

Time is valuable. Make sure that the times you do make an effort to go out that it's with someone who has been prescreened by a matchmaking service and therefore likely to be worth the time you took to leave your comfy sofa.

9. It's tough to date when you are shy or cautious, especially for women. When approached in a bar or social setting, you have no idea if the guy is married or just wanting to "get lucky." People that you meet through a matchmaking service are screened. You will know their marital status is never married, divorced, or widowed. They are guaranteed to be single and open to dating.

10. Once you're past your twenties, it seems like it gets harder and harder to meet people in your age group. More people are married or "hooked up," and the dating pool gets smaller, or at least it seems so. Matchmaking services have a wide array of members of various ages so you have access to available people in your own age group. When thirty-eight-year-old Ellen went to a singles group at her church, she found that she was the only member under the age of sixty! After joining a matchmaking service, Ellen is now meeting eligible men in her own age group.

Seven Things to Keep in Mind When Joining a Matchmaking Service

There are good and bad matchmaking services. Your time and money are precious, so ask questions before you sign up with a service. Don't be afraid to visit more than one until you find a service that feels right for you. Some things to check out are:

1. Compare prices. Both dating and matchmaking services can be quite expensive, but there are services to fit every budget. You can be sure if a company refuses to discuss price over the phone, it will be costly, usually in the thousands. Be careful and be sure to comparison shop. A benefit of choosing a fee-based service is that it may screen out people who are not serious about finding a long-term relationship. In other words, if they are willing to pay, they are more likely to be truly looking for a soul mate. In some cities, there are matchmaking services that do not charge the ladies as long as they meet certain criteria. Usually these services require that the woman look like a model.

2. Make sure that they have members in your part of town. Many services insist that members meet potential matches in other counties, cities, states, or even countries! Most people do not want a long-distance relationship.

3. Don't feel pressured by aggressive salespeople. Matchmaking and dating services are businesses. They want your patronage. Don't let them talk you into joining before they have answered all of your questions satisfactorily. And don't let yourself be conned by a salesperson saying that the price is only good if you join right now. That is a sales tactic.

4. Ask how long they have been in business and what their track record is. (However, they will never admit if they have a bad track record). Ask for testimonials from satisfied customers. Check with the Better Business Bureau to see if there have been complaints filed against them.

5. If you do join, read your contract! Know what you are getting yourself into. Most people don't even know what they have signed.

6. Make sure that you feel comfortable with your matchmaker. If you don't feel this person is really listening to your needs, don't hesitate to ask to work with someone else. Sometimes another personality will be a better fit for you.

7. Realize that the service can only match you to people they have in their database. Most places don't go out and do special searches for the right partner. They work with people who have come in and joined. You can tell them exactly what you are looking for, but if they don't have it, they don't have it. Also, you will never really know how many members they have, because most services exaggerate that aspect. So if you are too specific—for example, you want a Brad Pitt look-alike, over six feet tall, who makes a million a year, never married, no kids, wants kids, speaks French, loves teacup poodles, and can cook—well, good luck!

About the Author

 Marla was born in Tacoma, Washington, the "City of Destiny." Born with a natural flair for acting, she also had a deep interest in reading and writing poetry and short stories. At the age of sixteen, she was living in Iran with her family and learning to speak French and Persian. During the revolution in Iran, Marla's family moved back to Washington State, where she finished her last year in high school and one year in college.

After that, she moved to Hollywood to pursue an acting career, doing television commercials and print modeling. In the early 1990s, she moved to Chicago where she found that she could use her dating experience to help others. She has been working in Los Angeles as a matchmaker since 2001 and has successfully introduced many couples who have gotten married!

Marla's work inspires people and gives them hope that they can find their soul mate. Marla married her own in Mexico City in 2002. A world traveler and culture nut, Marla describes herself as having a French flair, a Persian heart, Italian fire, and Mexican taste buds!

Excuse Me, Your Life Is Now

Real-Life Transformations from
Excuse Me, Your Life Is Waiting

Doreen Banaszak

Lynn Grabhorn's wildly popular book, *Excuse Me, Your Life Is Waiting,* offered four fundamental principles for attracting what we desire most in life. Now Doreen Banaszak has created a sequel that not only presents a convenient review of Grabhorn's four basic tenets—identifying what we don't want, naming what we do want, getting into the feeling of what we want and, finally, allowing what we want to flow into our lives—but also offers overwhelming evidence that these principles really work!

Following Grabhorn's untimely death in 2004, Banaszak, who teaches the principles and has been inundated with true stories of transformation by Grabhorn's readers, assembled this fascinating collection of personal accounts of the principles in practice. These true stories explore the amazing ways that readers' lives have been transformed as these focused, highly motivated individuals put the principles to work to manifest their dreams. As they "got in touch with their feelings," they successfully replaced negative ones like fear, anxiety, and doubt with positive ones like joy, excitement, anticipation, and gratitude. This process allowed their dreams to manifest with astounding speed and clarity! These transformative tales are packed with irrefutable evidence of our magical power to create the life we desire—and detailed instructions on how to do it.

Paperback • 216 pages • ISBN 978-1-57174-543-9 • $15.95

Excuse Me, Your Job Is Waiting
Attract the Work You Want
Laura George

New York Times best-selling author Lynn Grabhorn showed half a million readers how to "magnetize" their emotions to draw their desires to them. Now, human resource manager Laura George applies Grabhorn's powerful Law of Attraction to the life experiences of both losing and getting a job. George captures the style and substance of *Excuse Me* and helps you identify the qualities you want in a job and then shows you how to flip the negative feelings you may be carrying ("the economy is terrible"; "I can't believe I got laid off"; "I'm too old") so you can stay focused and upbeat to draw that perfect job to you.

Experienced in job hunting from both sides of the interview table, George understands all the highs and lows in this emotionally draining process. As a job seeker, she teaches you to stay positive after months of few prospects and little hope. As a human resource manager, she also knows that these powerful, positive feelings can land seekers the job of their dreams. By exploring the "power of feelings" on your job search, this new job seeker's guide is unlike any other.

Paperback • ISBN 978-1-57174-529-3 • 312 pages • $16.95

Excuse Me, Your God Is Waiting

Love your god. Create your life. Find your true self.

Michelle Prosser

Conversations with God revolutionized the thoughts of millions by explaining how God wants us to create our lives and become the magnificent, powerful spiritual beings God intended. *Excuse Me, Your Life Is Waiting* inspired half a million readers to transform their lives through the "astonishing power" of positive feelings.

In *Excuse Me, Your Life Is Waiting*, corporate life coach Prosser connects the dots between your faith in God, your understanding of the Law of Attraction, and your ability to converse with God. When God is part of the equation, the success of attracting what you really want and becoming who you want to be expands exponentially.

Paperback • 192 pages • ISBN 978-1-57174-552-1 • $15.95

www.hrpub.com · 1-800-766-8009

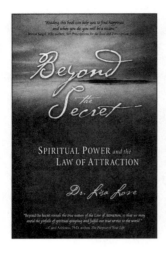

Beyond the Secret
Spiritual Power and the Law of Attraction
Dr. Lisa Love

The recent documentary and book, *The Secret,* took the Law of Attraction to a vast new audience. However, knowing about the secret is only the first step toward understanding how the Law of Attraction works and how we are meant to use it in a spiritual way. Using the Law of Attraction is not just about knowing how to call abundance into our lives. It is also about knowing at a soul-deep level what our Spirit deems good for us and therefore wants for us. Rarely do we get to keep that which our own Spirit has not already approved for us.

Beyond the Secret explains how to align with our own Spirit so we can use the very powerful Law of Attraction truthfully and securely—ensuring that what we wish for is actually good for self. When the Spirit approves of the abundance (love, health, wealth, whatever), then the spirit will guide it. This is the key to keeping what we want. We discover that attracted abundance contributes to ourselves, to the good of others, and to the collective consciousness of the world.

Paperback • ISBN 978-1-57174-556-9 • 216 pages • $15.95

The Excuse Me, Your Life Is Waiting *Playbook*

With the Twelve Tenets of Empowerment

Lynn Grabhorn

Human beings have evolved physically, socially, and technologically, but are unable to take the next step toward spiritual evolution because of self-defeating habits and conditioning—in short, we are our own victims. Lynn Grabhorn has taken the concepts that made *Excuse Me, Your Life Is Waiting* a bestseller and transformed them into a complete workbook for empowerment. The clearly focused explanations, discussion material, meditations, and exercises are essential building blocks to a new way of being. Isn't it worth a little work to have the life you've always wanted?

- Based on the principles of the self-help sensation *Excuse Me, Your Life Is Waiting*
- Ideal for group or individual study
- Crosses the boundaries of age, gender, race, income, and religious belief
- A straight-shooting, carefully orchestrated program for self-improvement

Trade paper • 288 pages • ISBN 1-57174-270-4 • $22.95

Hampton Roads Publishing Company

. . . for the evolving human spirit

bettie youngs books

HAMPTON ROADS PUBLISHING COMPANY publishes books
on a variety of subjects, including spirituality,
health, and other related topics.

For a copy of our latest trade catalog, call toll-free,
800-766-8009, or send your name and address to:

HAMPTON ROADS PUBLISHING COMPANY, INC.
1125 STONEY RIDGE ROAD • CHARLOTTESVILLE, VA 22902
e-mail: hrpc@hrpub.com • www.hrpub.com